Intimate Migra

Intimate Migrations

Gender, Family, and Illegality
among Transnational Mexicans

Deborah A. Boehm

NEW YORK UNIVERSITY PRESS
New York and London

NEW YORK UNIVERSITY PRESS
New York and London
www.nyupress.org

References to Internet websites (URLs) were accurate at the time of writing.
Neither the author nor New York University Press is responsible for URLs
that may have expired or changed since the manuscript was prepared.

Library of Congress Cataloging-in-Publication Data
Boehm, Deborah A.
Intimate migrations : gender, family, and illegality among transnational Mexicans / Deborah A. Boehm.
    p. cm.
Includes bibliographical references and index.
ISBN 978-0-8147-8983-4 (cloth : acid-free paper)
ISBN 978-0-8147-8985-8 (ebook)
ISBN 978-0-8147-8986-5 (ebook)
1. Mexicans — United States — Social conditions.
2. Mexican Americans — Social conditions.
3. Immigrants — United States — Social conditions.
4. Transnationalism. 5. Sex role — United States.
6. Mexican American families. 7. Immigrant families — United States.
8. Illegal aliens — United States.
9. United States — Emigration and immigration — Social aspects.
10. Mexico — Emigration and immigration — Social aspects. I. Title.
E184.M5B59 2012
304.8'73072 — dc23
                          2011043847

New York University Press books are printed on acid-free paper,
and their binding materials are chosen for strength and durability.
We strive to use environmentally responsible suppliers and materials
to the greatest extent possible in publishing our books.

Manufactured in the United States of America
10 9 8 7 6 5 4 3 2 1

For Ava, and in loving memory of my grandmother,
Lufteria Gabona Christie Boehm,
the first immigrant to tell me her story.

Contents

We are from both sides—from here and from there.
I suppose we are from two places.

—Victor

I think that I am divided . . . I think of home as half there,
half here.

—Lucía

I wander about . . . I am from neither here nor there!

—Ofelia

Acknowledgments

As a child, I was often shown a photograph of my grandmother and her family—immigrants from Macedonia—taken in the early twentieth century when my grandmother was just four years old. The family is gathered together, staring at the camera with serious expressions, a reflection of the poverty, war, and survival that defined their lives. But this photograph of a family united is an illusion of sorts: the image was created transnationally. A photograph of my great-grandmother and her children was taken in a town close to their small village that is now part of Greece; this was joined with another photograph of my great-grandfather and my grandmother's eldest brother, taken years before the family was actually reunited, at a small studio in Portland, Oregon. It was an attempt to reunite those in the homeland, at least visually, with the men in the family who had already migrated to the United States. The photograph, especially the story behind it, made an impression, and as I have conducted research with transnational Mexicans, the image and its sentiment have stayed with me.

While there are parallels between the migration experiences of my family and those of transnational Mexicans—many of which I explore in this book, including divided and reunited kin, the distinctly gendered aspects of movement, and the effect of migration on people of all ages including children—there are also striking differences. My grandmother and her family arrived by ship to New York City and, after an immigration official changed their surname, they were sent on their way and boarded a train west. This is, of course, quite different from the border crossings of Mexican migrants into the United States in recent decades. My great-grandparents and my grandmother became U.S. citizens through a relatively simple process, and in a manner essentially impossible for the migrants I know. I hope that readers will situate this account of Mexican migration within a historical and cross-cultural frame, recognizing the similarities with previous migrations to the United States, but also the distinct circumstances that Mexican nationals face in the early twenty-first century. I am grateful to my late grandmother for sharing the stories of her migration, as they have directed and continue to guide my work.

Although my research has personal beginnings, it is the product of years of scholarship and has been shaped by exchanges with many mentors, colleagues, and students. I want to recognize the talented and devoted teachers who have contributed to different stages of my education and fostered my own dedication to becoming an educator. I thank my doctoral committee—Louise Lamphere, Carole Nagengast, Sylvia Rodríguez, and the late Michael Kearney—and scholars who have commented on my work at different times and provided mentorship and guidance: Leo Chavez, Susan Coutin, Yen Le Espiritu, Elzbieta Goździak, Joe Heyman, Gail Mummert, Roger Rouse, Louisa Schein, Dianna Shandy, Lynn Stephen, and Susan Terrio. I have also had the good fortune of working closely with many individuals as co-author and co-editor, and I thank these friends and colleagues, including Bianet Castellanos, Cati Coe, Julia Meredith Hess, Heather Rae-Espinoza, Rachel Reynolds, and Heidi Swank.

I appreciate the many opportunities for exchange with scholars and friends in both Mexico and the United States. I thank those I have met during classes, seminars, writing groups, workshops, and fellowships: Jeanette Acosta, Carina Alencar, Jiemin Bao, Judy Boruchoff, Beth Buggenhagen, Nancy Burke, Mónica Díaz, Joanna Dreby, Tory Gavito, Nora Haenn, Sarah Horton, David Martin, Héctor Mendoza, Mariela Nuñez-Janes, Ethan Sharp, Karen Stocker, and Rachael Stryker. I also thank Olga Giller and Michael Ramos, my co-teachers in Albuquerque, ex-pats Mark and Patricia Dunn, and Rita McGary, a tireless advocate for migrants. My time at the Center for U.S.-Mexican Studies and the Center for Comparative Immigration Studies at the University of California–San Diego was particularly fruitful, and I am grateful for this invaluable support. Thanks to Wayne Cornelius for creating this special place for scholarship, and to those I met during my residency, including Fernando Alanis, Xavi Escandell, Lieba Faier, Gaby Sandoval, Suzanne Simon, Maria Tapias, Gaku Tsuda, and Carolyn Pinedo Turnovsky.

Several organizations have provided funding and support that made this project possible. My experience as a WorldTeach volunteer in Guayaquil, Ecuador, introduced me to and fostered my interest in Latin America. During graduate studies at the University of New Mexico, I received grants from a number of departments and organizations: a Foreign Language and Area Studies (FLAS) Title VI Fellowship; PhD Fellowships from the Latin American and Iberian Institute and the Center for Regional Studies; the Bunting Award from the Department of Anthropology; and research and travel grants from the Department of Anthropology, Department of Family and Community Medicine, Graduate and Professional Student Association, Latin American and Iberian Institute, Office of Graduate Studies, Southwest Hispanic Research Institute, and Women Studies Program. A David L. Boren Graduate International Fellowship from the Academy of Educational Development provided essential funding for dissertation research.

I appreciate a Transnationalism Fellowship from the Mexico-North Research Network and the opportunity to work with Federico Besserer from the Universidad Autónoma Metropolitana–Iztapalapa. A travel grant at the University of Nevada–Las Vegas enabled fieldwork in 2007. I was grateful to receive a Fulbright-García Robles Fellowship in 2010 and thus spend a year based at the Universidad Autónoma de Zacatecas as I was completing the manuscript. Special thanks to Miguel Moctezuma Longoria for the invitation to spend the year there, and to Raúl Delgado Wise and everyone at the Estudios del Desarrollo for being so welcoming. My research has also benefited from a seminar at the Colegio de México's Programa Interdisciplinario de Estudios de la Mujer, the Social Science Research Council's Summer Institute on International Migration at the University of California–Los Angeles, and a Wenner-Gren Workshop in New York City on childhood and migration.

I am especially grateful to my current institution, the University of Nevada–Reno, for ongoing support of my research through a Junior Faculty Research Grant, Scholarly and Creative Activity Grants, summer and travel support, and leave during 2010 to conduct fieldwork in Mexico. I so appreciate my colleagues in my two academic homes, the Department of Anthropology and the Women's Studies Program, and the engaging intellectual community of faculty associates in Gender, Race, and Identity Studies. I value their collegiality, mentorship, and humor. Special thanks to Nadine Attewell and Brett Van Hoesen, members of my junior faculty cohort. I thank the students I have learned from, and I particularly recognize those in a Fall 2009 course about gender and migration for their commitment to this important topic. I also value my friends outside of academia, especially Christine Seethaler for being a trusted friend over the years.

I am very appreciative of Alyshia Gálvez for introducing me to Jennifer Hammer, my wonderful editor at NYU Press. I thank Jennifer for her guidance and support, and thanks to her, Gabrielle Begue, and Despina Papazoglou Gimbel for their professionalism. I also appreciate the thoughtful comments provided by two anonymous reviewers, and thank you to Jeffrey H. Cohen for reading the completed manuscript. Many thanks to Antonio Vigil for allowing his work to be featured on the book's cover, and for sharing such insight about migration and border crossings through his art. My experience with NYU Press has been a pleasure each step of the way, and for this I am sincerely grateful.

I wish to acknowledge my family, some of the most influential teachers I have had. I am indebted to my parents, Robert and Marcia Boehm, who have provided unfailing support, and cultivated a love of learning as well as a commitment to public education and social justice—I cannot thank them enough. Sincere thanks to my brother, Chris Boehm, who inspires me. And, thank you to my husband's family, the Jackson-Kelly-Rousseau clan. I was fortunate to join them, and I value their collective wit, creativity, and sense of adventure. I am especially grateful for my exceptional partner and friend, Patrick Jackson, who embraces each day with humor, spontaneity, and optimism, and without whom I could not have carried out this research. Much love to our sparkling daughter and fieldwork companion, Ava, whose arrival and childhood have been intertwined with this project.

Above all, I thank the transnational Mexicans who made my research possible. I am deeply grateful to these "ethnographic interlocutors" (De Genova 1999), many of them close friends or kin through *compadrazgo* [co-parenting], who have welcomed me into their homes, shared their experiences, provided feedback, and, ultimately, guided my research. While I would like to recognize them each individually, current political realities—the very subject of this book—prevent me from doing so, and so I use pseudonyms for collaborators and communities, as well as change identifying details throughout the book. I particularly thank the students in my ESL and U.S. citizenship classes, those who first introduced me to individuals living in San Marcos, and migrants who have hosted me and my family in their homes. I very much appreciate the many candid exchanges I have had with transmigrants in the United States and residents of ranchos in Mexico. In one especially memorable conversation, after discussing the dangers migrants face crossing the border, a woman emphatically told me, "*That* is the story you should include in your *reportaje* [your "report," as writings about my research became known]." As exemplified in the transnational photograph of my grandmother and family, there are a multitude of rich stories about the intimate lives of (im)migrants that are worth sharing, many of which are not as straightforward as they might initially appear. I hope that I have indeed included the important ones.

Introduction

De Ambos Lados / From Both Sides

Rancho San Marcos, San Luis Potosí, México. On one of my first days conducting fieldwork in rural Mexico, I found myself looking at a painted photograph of a handsome young man with chiseled features. The yellowed edges of the photo showed its age, and there was a jagged crack in the glass cover. The woman I was visiting, Ofelia, walked in and saw me studying the photo. "That is my late husband, God bless him. He was a good man. That photograph was taken when he was eighteen years old, just weeks before he left for the United States as a bracero," she explained. She then pointed around the room to several other large photographs of family members who were living in the United States. "That is my daughter-in-law, Mario's wife, on their wedding day." The bride was wearing a tiara, surrounded by a cloud of white toile. "The first time I went to the United States was when I traveled to New Mexico for their wedding ceremony." "That," she nodded toward a huge photo of a young man in western wear, "is my son Tomás. He hasn't been home for nearly four years. He went *como mojado* [without state authorization, literally "as a wetback" but without the negative connotations in English] so it is difficult for him to return to the rancho." In the photo, Tomás was in a felt cowboy hat; at his waist, a belt buckle with two interlacing horseshoes. "For luck," she explained, "because it is hard to be in the United States without documents."

After a moment, she continued: "And here is my granddaughter, Lila, at her *quinceañera* [fifteenth birthday party] in Albuquerque." Lila looked like a miniature bride, in a long white dress with pink silk flowers placed throughout her hair, a delicate gold cross necklace around her neck. "Today, seven of my children live in Albuquerque," Ofelia told me as she looked at the photographs around the room. "Like their father, my sons crossed the border for the first time when they were young, in search of work to make a living. Now several of my daughters have migrated as well. I have even waded through the Rio Grande myself," she said. "My late husband never would have imagined it!" She paused, and was silent as she glanced at each of the portraits, "Yes, there have been many changes since my husband first went to the United States so many years ago. It is hard to believe."

Albuquerque, New Mexico, United States Just weeks before departing for Mexico, I had visited Ofelia's daughter Lucía and her husband, Victor, in a recently purchased house in Albuquerque, where they were hosting a third birthday party—an important milestone among Mexicans—for their son, Carlito. Lucía greeted me at the door, "*¡Bienvenida!* Please, come inside. Can you believe how different it is from our apartment?!" Lucía asked, referring to a small two-bedroom apartment they had rented before the move. "After fourteen years, we finally have our own place." There were more than fifty family members in attendance, including Ofelia's children, grandchildren, and even great-grandchildren. The television was on, although no one seemed to be watching it; a small metallic banner, *Feliz Cumpleaños*, was draped above it. Several men were seated around the dining room table—some of Victor's and Lucía's brothers, as well as several cousins. There was another group of men in the backyard, overseeing the preparation of *carnitas* in a small firepit they had built. Children were running around, and several were jumping on a trampoline.

Lucía guided me into the kitchen, where nearly twenty women and girls filled the room. They greeted me and continued their conversation about a cousin's upcoming wedding and the recent deportation of a family friend. "It has been such a struggle for his wife," Lucía explained to me. "Can you imagine? Three young children, no income, such uncertainty about the future." The women whispered about the recent behavior of a community member—he bought a truck, had been going to shows, and had been staying out late drinking. There were even rumors that he was seeing another woman, especially scandalous given that he and his common-law wife had a newborn baby. The women were interrupted occasionally when someone ran a plate of food and a glass of orange soda out to a newcomer, but they picked up where they left off as soon as she returned. They heaped food onto a plate for me and protested when I did not eat it all. Lucía's sister Zulema looked around the room as she described her large family, "We don't even need friends, we have so many family members . . . and this is a small celebration!" she told me, laughing.

The partygoers were fascinated to hear that I would be visiting the rancho, their home, and they prepared me for my arrival by offering advice for my stay. "The rancho is isolated, there is nothing there," Lucía told me. "But I love it, I miss it. I often dream of living there again." Lucía's sister-in-law, who was born in the United States, recounted how she had to walk out in the corral, next to the pigs and goats, to go to the bathroom during her first visits to San Marcos. "I demanded that my husband buy his mother a toilet," she said. "So, fortunately, you will have a bathroom when you stay at my mother-in-law's house!" One of Lucía's brothers told me that I should make a trip out to the *milpas* soon after arriving. "It is beautiful, very peaceful. The beans will be nearly ready for harvest when you go." Lucía's son provided a lengthy description of the animals at his grandmother's home—pigs, goats, dogs, a horse. "If you go with my grandmother when she feeds them," he assured me, "you will be able to see them all." Finally, Lucía's teenage daughter, Cora, pulled me aside and warned me about the rancho. Her face was very close to mine as she whispered that it can be "soooo boring there." She added that despite how quiet the rancho is, she hoped to visit her grandmother sometime in the upcoming year, so perhaps we would have a chance to see each another in Mexico.

When I left the party late in the evening, Lucía had Victor carry a box out to my car. The box was filled with gifts for her mother and other family members, including clothes and shoes, some toys, and a small television. Lucía and Victor made small talk, and then there was a pause. "I wish we could go with you to our home," Lucía said longingly. "Well, to *one* of our homes," she added, looking back at her newly purchased house. "We are *de ambos lados* [from both sides]—from here and from there," joked Victor. "I suppose we are from two places."

In my work with transnational Mexicans, I have often asked individuals to imagine a scenario in which there are no barriers to movement between Mexico and the United States, and then I ask them where they would choose to live.[1] Almost always, Mexican (im)migrants tell me they would prefer the freedom to "go and come [*ir y venir*]," that ideally they would like to be in both countries and to create lives that are, as Victor described, "from both sides." Yet while there are transnational Mexicans who do move back and forth to create homes in both places, the barriers preventing such movement are many. The presence of the U.S. state is strong in everyday lives, evident through the categories that define and exclude members of the nation, as well as growing border controls, an increasing number of deportations of Mexican nationals, and shifting U.S. immigration policies.

Such processes limit cross-border movement, so that even if one does "go and come," it can be with months, years, or even decades between migrations north or south. And for all Mexican nationals, including those who have naturalized as or were born U.S. citizens, there are factors that prevent them from leading a life characterized by fluid, unrestricted movement between Mexico and the United States. Different subjectivities, experiences, and circumstances—based on legal status, as well as age, gender, sexuality, socioeconomic class, access to resources, race/ethnicity, marital status, and family ties—intersect with political-economic realities, shaping who migrates; if, when, and how often they do so; and the character of their border crossings and lengths of stay in the United States.

This book explores the intersection of intimacy and "illegality," uncovering the everyday experiences of migrant families—spaces that are often understood as domestic or private—as well as the public state actions that penetrate family life in multiple ways. Transnational Mexicans experience what I understand to be "intimate migrations," flows that both shape and are structured through gendered and familial actions and interactions, but are always defined by the presence of the U.S. state. The following chapters explore how state-regulated migration and migrants' emic understandings of family position, gendered selves, and generation are intertwined. Contextualizing today's transnational movement within migration trajectories of the past, it is clear that ostensibly "intimate" relations—in the sense of personal, close, familial—have long been shaped by the state's power to categorize migrants.

One's U.S. immigration status, and what anthropologist Nicholas De Genova identifies as "the legal production of migrant 'illegality'" (De Genova 2002: 419), is a constant backdrop to the intimate dimensions of transnational migration. Following De Genova and others (e.g., Coutin 2000; Chavez 2007; De Genova 2002; De Genova and Peutz 2010; Ngai 2004; Willen 2007), I problematize the very notion of "illegality" and aim to "de-naturalize the reification" of categories such as "legal," "illegal," and "alien" (Peutz and De Genova 2010: 3). Thus, these terms are used throughout the book with the recognition that they are constructions that reflect particular historical and political conditions rather than absolute or natural categories. The effects of such constructions are, of course, profound, and a principal goal of my work is to demonstrate the inaccuracy and inadequacy of this system of classification that shapes virtually all discourse about and experiences of (im)migration in the United States today.

Drawing on scholarship across disciplines, this book engages theories of transnationality and borderlands, state power and the construction of illegality, gender relations, family and kinship, childhood, and transnational intimacies. The ethnographic study of transnational migration reveals much about both the structuring of intimate lives and state power, and especially how state controls manifest in the everyday experiences of transnational Mexican women, men, and children. In much research about migration, intimate relationships go largely unnoticed. By demonstrating how intimate relations direct migration, and by examining kin and gender relationships explicitly through the lens of "illegality," this research offers a new approach to the study of the state, transnational migration, and intimate interactions.

While this project is informed by multidisciplinary research, it is also an ethnography that considers questions central to cultural anthropology. The book makes as its point of departure the "cultural logics" (Ong 1999) of gender and family that migrants embrace, reject, and/or reconfigure as they interact with state structures in a transnational space. It focuses on exchanges that are uniquely interpreted through ethnographic research: kinship and the (re)production of families; gendered subjectivities and relations; constructions of age and movement through the life cycle; and the character of negotiations between individuals and state regimes. Each of these intersecting lines of inquiry advances our understanding of the workings of kinship, gender, and age/generation, but also transnationality, state power, and "illegality."

Between Here and There

When Victor described his family as "from both sides—from here and from there," he was also articulating the notion of existing "in-between" (Bhabha 1994:1; Schuck 1998). Certainly, for transnational (im)migrants, there are "multiple 'heres' and 'theres'" (Sirkeci 2009: 4), "restless movement" that is "here and there, on all sides, *fort/da*, hither and thither, back and forth" (Bhabha 1994: 1). For example, while some immigrants may conceive of "the other side" as the homeland (e.g., Gabaccia 1994), transnational Mexicans understand "the other side" to be the destination. These "moving targets" (Appadurai 1989) are clearly relational and situational, much like the many ties and divisions among partners, family members, and adults and children that are described throughout this book. Close attention to the contexts within which people move or not reveals the intersection of spatiality and belonging, and demonstrates how transnational Mexicans are often caught between here and there, whether as a person walking across the border, an individual in the United States yearning for "home," the partner of a migrant who has never been to the other side, or a child who is sent north or south by family members.

Transnational Mexican migrants use decidedly spatial terms to depict movement and their "place" in the world—territorial locales as well as symbolic spaces of membership and exclusion. Migrants understand themselves as belonging to, divided between, and outside of two nation-states: here and there. (Im)migrants are, in their own words, "*de ambos lugares*/from both places" and "*de ambos lados*/from both sides," "*mitad allá, mitad aquí*/half there, half here," "*del otro lado*/from the other side," and, tellingly, "*ni de aquí, ni de allá*/from neither here nor there." While transnational movement makes "geographical and territorial certainties seem increasingly fragile" (Appadurai 1989: i), place matters even as it is transcended (Boehm 2010). Transnational subjects do not experience "placelessness" (Appadurai 1989: iii) as much as a "(re)construction of 'place' or locality" in which "points of origin" are "transferred and regrounded" (Vertovec 2009: 12). Guided by research participants, my analysis of transnational migration is indeed rooted in places but also, centrally, captures how lives extend beyond particular locations.

The theme of place as geographic locale but also as a metaphor for position, experience, or situation (see Feld and Basso 1996) runs throughout the book. The narratives of transnational Mexicans capture the contradictions of migration and separation—going and staying, connections and divisions, movement and its obstacles—and are powerful descriptions of the experiences of transnational Mexicans as they go and do not go between Mexico and the United States. Recognizing the problematic character of "either/or tropes" (Bailey 2009: 80), I write against the lure to "place" people geographically and conceptually as either here or there. Such work challenges the widely accepted and "decidedly modern" notion of the "excluded middle," that is, the idea that someone or something must "be here or there, but not in both places at once" (see Pollock et al. 2002: 11–12). Significantly, the assumption of an "excluded middle" permeates much more than conceptions of place; it drives policies, defines the U.S. categorization of (im)migrants, and perpetuates profound social injustice. Indeed, forcing transnational Mexicans into particular categories and "places" appears to be one of the U.S. state's guiding projects.

In addition to questioning the here–there binary, this book complicates multiple conceptual divides of the current moment—including public–private, intimate–structural, individual–collective, immigrant–nonimmigrant, man–woman, and adult–child—to consider how transnational Mexicans experience locations and positions as both, neither, divided, and/or between. It is through these situated depictions of (im)migrants' everyday lives that I develop an analysis of the nexus of intimacy and state power. Close consideration of kinship, gender, and generation in transnational perspective shows how individuals and families are divided and united (part I), captures the fluidity and disruptions within gendered kin relations (part II), and demonstrates the simultaneity of belonging and exclusion that increasingly defines the lives of transnational Mexicans of all ages (part III). Tracing the "interactional wear and tear involved in this daily work of reproduction in a diasporic world" (Appadurai 1989: iii–iv), this ethnography portrays the character of state power as Mexican (im)migrants interact with family members; form, sustain, and/or dissolve partnerships across the U.S.-Mexico border; and negotiate with parents, children, and caregivers—transnational lives that are, in many ways, between here and there.

Placing Intimate Migrations

"My husband must migrate soon . . . he needs to join his brothers on the other side." As we spoke, Mariela was in her home in the rancho, preparing the midday meal. The kitchen was small and tidy—the concrete floor had just been mopped and the scent of bleach was strong. In one corner, there was a bright yellow stove and a dishwashing station, and in the other, a refrigerator that had not been running for nearly two days since the power had gone out. Mariela is young, in her late twenties, with three children, ages ten, five, and two. With the back of her wrist, she dabbed at the tears welling up in her eyes. "I don't want us to live apart, but we really don't have any other options. Unless he wants to start a business . . . we could move to Monterrey and he could sell food or housewares in the market. But my husband is a farmer, what does he know about running a business? I am pressuring him to go to the other side. I take care of all my responsibilities—the house, the children, cooking, cleaning. I even make tamales and sell them—this brings great shame to my husband, but what else can I do? Now he must take care of his responsibilities for my sake, for our family. We just don't have enough money to get by."

That night, after talking with Mariela, I wrote about the inseparability of gender, family, and migration in the lives of transnational Mexicans. I was struck by the ways that an intimate, everyday, and seemingly insignificant family negotiation in an "out-of-the-way place" (Tsing 1993) was decisively connected to the sweeping, large-scale forces of transnationalism and global movement. This was one of many conversations I had over a period of years—with women as they shopped in grocery stores in the United States, with men in front of *tiendas* in small towns in Mexico, with teenagers as they attended dances, with children at family gatherings, and with elders talking of the past and future—that repeatedly brought me back to a premise that runs throughout the book and informs each chapter: the overlapping spheres of state power and intimate lives cannot be separated.

The experiences of Mariela's family emphasize this point. Although Mariela and her husband have never been to the United States, the U.S.

state is ever present, affecting decisions they will make about the possibility and viability of future migrations. If her husband goes, it is likely that he will migrate alone or with other men from the community. He would migrate without papers, crossing a dangerous and highly militarized international border. If he successfully crosses, he will live in the United States as an unauthorized migrant, marginalized and vulnerable, joining millions of undocumented migrants who live with "deportability" (De Genova 2002), or a constant threat of deportation. If Mariela and her children migrate north at some point in the future to reunite the family, they, too, will interact with the U.S. state and immigration laws in particular ways, mediated by gender and age. Whether members of this family migrate or not, the shadow of "illegality" will remain. These are intimate migrations that are situated between here and there, directed by gendered and familial relationships, and always shaped by state power and the production of (il)legality.

Mapping Intimate Migrations

It is in these geographic, conceptual, and lived spaces between the intimate and the structural that intimate migrations are constituted. The study of intimate migrations challenges the "overly binary models of . . . intimate and impersonal" (Constable 2009: 57), especially by questioning the "public/private mirage" (Bhattacharjee 2006). Recognizing that "everyday encounters with the state . . . have increasingly dissolved the boundaries between 'public' and 'private' spheres" (Maira 2009: 26; see also Yuval-Davis and Werbner 1999: 29), I study state actions precisely through the intimate interactions of everyday life. This is an approach that takes "the creation of specific kinds of subjects and bodies to be fundamental to the making of a body politic" (Stoler 2002: 9). In other words, experiences on the ground cannot be separated from state policies and practices that are in turn constituted by the actions of transnational migrants.

This book builds on and contributes to an emergent literature about desire and intimacy in transnational context, work that collectively challenges researchers to bridge analyses of macro forces with ethnographic studies of interpersonal relationships (e.g., Brennan 2004; Cantú 2009; Constable 2003; Ehrenreich and Hochschild 2002; Faier 2007, 2009; Gopinath 2005; Hirsch 2003; Manalansan 2003; Padilla et al. 2008; Povinelli 2006; Wilson 2004). Like colonial contexts (e.g., Stoler 1995, 2002), today's state regimes shape gendered family life, and intimate exchanges are always structured by and situated within social and economic processes (Lamphere 1992; Lamphere,

Ragoné, and Zavella 1997). Global capital is intertwined with intimate relations and identities (Wilson 2004) and transnational "encounters" are both deeply personal and embedded in broader relations of power (Faier 2009). An ethnographic view reveals how intimate relations motivate, guide, and are directed by global migrations, directly linking gendered kin relations to global processes.

At the center of my analysis are emic, cultural understandings of the intimate—that which is perceived as familiar or personal (see Faier 2009; Wilson 2004)—and the ways that such relations both shape and are shaped by migration. This process is dialectical, one in which intimate selves and relations guide migration, and wherein transnational movement is changing multiple subjectivities. Although dimensions of the self have often been perceived as marginal to global migrations (see Mahler and Pessar 2006), intimate relations and labor migrations cannot be separated from one another within the realities of everyday lives. Tracing various gendered kin relationships—between partners, parents and children, and family members—underscores and clarifies this point in transnational perspective.

My research is part of a theoretical move to rethink notions of family within migration flows. Mexican migration has been guided by family relations since the 1800s (Alvarez 1987). Across international boundaries and over time, "family" takes various forms, including "transnational" or "binational" families (Chavez 1992: 121, 128) in which members are divided by distance yet maintain ties through travel and migration, communications, and remittances. Anthropology, arguably more than any field, has enhanced understandings of relatedness, and ethnography uniquely reveals the nuances of family life. This book builds on literature that examines how family is structured and restructured over time, the constant and changing forms of family relations in migrant communities, and the multiple meanings of kinship that emerge in a global context (e.g., Cole and Durham 2007; Dreby 2010; Foner 2009; Glick Schiller and Fouron 2001; Levitt 2001; Menjívar 2000; Newendorp 2008; Olwig 2007; Ong 1999; Wilson 2009; Zimmerman, Litt, and Bose 2006). A reconsideration of kinship demonstrates how family relations are maintained, (re)constituted, and/or transformed through transnational migration.

Within a transnational space, gender politics direct migrations and determine who goes and who stays. Over the past decades, an analysis of gender has moved "from the periphery toward the core of migration studies" (Mahler and Pessar 2006). The sociologist Pierrette Hondagneu-Sotelo (2003a) has identified different stages of research about gender and global movement, beginning with an absence of literature about women, and the assumption that migrants are male and migration therefore affects only men. In the 1970s, feminists shifted inquiry to focus on "the immigrant woman" and later, immigrant women (e.g., Gabaccia 1992; Lamphere 1987; Pozzetta 1991), although analysis continued to consider women and men as separate categories. Beginning in the 1990s, especially with Hondagneu-Sotelo's *Gendered Transitions* (1994), the field was defined by the "engendering" (Pessar 1999; 2003) of migration studies, with the introduction of a perspective that continues today: gender as constructed, relational, and fluid.

Currently, building on previous feminist anthropological inquiry (e.g., Behar and Gordon 1995; Rosaldo and Lamphere 1974), the end is no longer explicating women's experiences; instead, a focus on women serves as the means to gain insights about gender through the study of the actions and experiences of both women and men. The growing literature on gender and migration has shifted analysis from the study of unmarked men and later "women," to "gender" as inherently negotiated (e.g., Boehm and Castellanos 2008; Donato et al. 2006; Hirsch 2003; Hondagneu-Sotelo 1994; 1999b; 2003b; Mahler and Pessar 2001b; Pessar 1999; Pessar and Mahler 2003; Segura and Zavella 2007). Emergent research on gender and global movement is often informed by a transnational feminist frame (e.g., Alarcón, Kaplan, and Moallem 1999; Alexander and Mohanty 1997; Grewal and Kaplan 1994; Kaplan, Alarcón, and Moallem 1999), which extends earlier feminist analyses through a specific focus on structural, and especially (post)colonial, processes. These are "gendered geographies of power" (Mahler and Pessar 2001a) within which gendered interactions can be traced transnationally.

The ethnographic study of young people and migration is also growing, and several recent collections study the topic (e.g., Coe et al. 2011; Cole and Durham 2007, 2008; Ensor and Goździak 2010; Knörr 2005; Maira and Soep 2005). Scholars have researched the ways that parents and others perceive migration as affecting children (e.g., Dreby 2006, 2010; Gamburd 2000; Hondagneu-Sotelo 2007; Hondagneu-Sotelo and Avila 1997; Menjívar and Abrego 2009; Parreñas 2005), outlining how global flows result in transnational parenting and caregiving arrangements in which children stay—or are "left behind" as it is often problematically labeled by researchers—in the country of origin while their parents migrate to other countries to work. Much of this literature has focused on the experiences of mothers migrating and the impact of feminized migration on families and children in different contexts around the globe, including, for example, migration from Mexico to the United States (Dreby 2010; Hondagneu-Sotelo 2007), from Sri Lanka to countries in the Middle East (Gamburd 2000), and from the Philippines to the United States and Europe (Parreñas 2001, 2005, 2008). Such scholarship also emphasizes broad shifts in care patterns across generations (Zimmerman, Litt, and Bose 2006) and along lines of gender (Cole and Durham 2007; Dreby 2010; Parreñas 2005, 2008), underscoring how global labor relations inevitably affect relationships between children and caregivers.

While migrants' perspectives on family, gender, and children are central to this book, the other significant frame focuses on structural power, emphasizing how the production of illegality shapes and can overshadow family relations, gendered interactions, and exchanges across generations. For those whose lives transcend national borders, the state penetrates nearly every gendered and familial exchange. Notions and expressions of kinship and gender that direct migration are repeatedly mediated by one's position as a transnational subject—whether an individual has ever migrated or not—and especially the ways that (im)migrants are categorized by the U.S. state. The U.S. state's presence in what may be understood as the "intimate" or "personal" lives of transnational Mexicans is palpable, even in situations in which this may not be initially evident or appear to be the case. It is in the everyday lives and quotidian acts of migrants that the state's presence is strong, including, for example, the negotiations of a couple living in different countries, the daily routine or trials of a family living without documents in the United States, or the lives of U.S. citizen children living with a grandmother or aunt in Mexico.

To understand the nexus of intimate and state spheres, then, this book bridges work on gender, family, and migration with scholarship focused on the construction of (il)legality. This literature about illegality considers the contradictory ways that state regimes construct "legal" and "illegal" subjects and unpacks state categories as people cross nation-state borders (e.g., Chavez 1992, 2001, 2008; Coutin 2000, 2007; De Genova 2002, 2005a, 2005b; De Genova and Peutz 2010; Ngai 2004; Willen 2007). Focusing on the historical, political, and social context within which states create illegality, scholars have uncovered the processes and mechanisms through which such categories are constructed. However, few ethnographers have focused on how state strategies penetrate family life and the effect of legal categorization within gendered exchanges and among people of different ages. An aim of this ethnography is to bring together distinct bodies of work to understand the effect of such categorization within intimate migrations.

The experiences of transnational Mexicans demonstrate the state's potency and reach, as well as the state's inability to completely define personal lives.

While I consider the intimate interactions of migrants, this is, above all, an ethnography of how supposedly "personal" lives cannot be extracted from, and must be considered within the context of, state power. One's status vis-à-vis the state as citizen–noncitizen, man–woman, or adult–child interacts with, contradicts, and at times undermines migrants' understandings of gender subjectivities, family position, and relatedness. By focusing on this complicated, nuanced, and often messy, process—how intimate relations shift and endure in global migrations—I demonstrate the many ways that state regimes affect gender relations and restructure kinship among migrants and even those living outside of the state's borders.

Intimate Histories and Policies

Intimate migrations are historically rooted, and can be traced through overlapping political, economic, and familial relationships. In addition, the current moment is a defining one. The Mexican states of Zacatecas and San Luis Potosí, the focus of this research, have been characterized by migration to the United States for most of the past century, a legacy that has directly informed current gendered patterns of movement and created family lives that span the U.S-Mexico Border. Today, the U.S. state's reach into the intimate lives of transnational Mexicans is evident in increasing and often unsettling ways: couples, parents, children, and siblings are divided (see chaps. 2 and 3); gendered politics are being (re)constituted as a result of migrations (chap. 4), especially those that are not authorized by the U.S. state (chap. 5); children, from infants to teenagers, are increasingly crossing the U.S.-Mexico border without documents (chap. 6); and the parents of U.S. citizen children are being deported or sending their children to Mexico because of fear of deportation (chap. 7).

Mexican nationals make up the largest number of authorized and unauthorized (im)migrants in the United States, and they account for the largest group of (im)migrants naturalizing as U.S. citizens (U. S. Department of Homeland Security 2010; Passel and Cohn 2010). Mexican (im)migration to the United States has been defined by ambiguities and inconsistencies, the result of more than a century of shifting U.S. immigration policies and practices (see Massey, Durand, and Malone 2002): systematic labor recruitment beginning in the 1800s; the massive repatriation of Mexican nationals in the 1920s and 1930s; the Bracero Program (1942–64); "Operation Wetback" (1954); contradictory legislation such as the Immigration Reform and Control Act (IRCA) of 1986 and the Illegal Immigration Reform and Individual Responsibility Act (IIRIRA) of 1996; post-9/11 border "security" acts; and a recent rise in deportations of foreign nationals. The U.S. Congress continues to discuss the possibility of immigration reform even as the nation's borders are fortified in the name of "national security." Despite U.S. efforts to decrease (im)migration from Mexico, Mexican nationals continue to come to the United States (Passel 2005; Spener 2009), and U.S. immigration controls are, in fact, encouraging longer stays among unauthorized migrants (Cornelius 2006).

Since preconquest, the Americas have been characterized by the flow of people and the exchange of objects (Vélez-Ibáñez 1996: 22). Today, migra-tions—of capital and products, symbols and ideas, and most significantly, people—continue, and the U.S.-Mexico borderlands are characterized by constant movement and exchange. However, "migrations are produced" through "political, military, and economic links" (Sassen 1996b: 225, 218) and reflect a profound imbalance of power that plays out in the everyday lives of transnational migrants. The intimacy of transnationality has been and con-tinues to be characterized by both continuity and fragmentation: flows, con-nections, and linkages characterize transnational lives as do breaks, shifts, dislocations, and disruptions (see Appadurai 2006; Inda and Rosaldo 2008; Kearney 2004; Ong 2003; Ong and Collier 2005; Tsing 2005). State power penetrates intimate lives, creating fissures, "friction" (Tsing 2005), and woes (Parreñas 2005), and yet, lives go on: intimate migrations are "everyday ruptures" (Coe et al. 2011), through which disruption and consistency are simultaneous.

Whether or not they include an explicit focus on gender and family, U.S. immigration policies and practices have shaped intimate migrations. For example, the Bracero Program played a fundamental role in creating the present character of migration (see also Chavez 1992; Hondagneu-Sotelo 1994; Stephen 2007). Through this program the U.S. state contracted with male laborers, initiating a pattern of primarily male migration from multiple regions throughout Mexico that persists today. The gendering of migration continued under IRCA, which allowed individuals who could document continuous residency in the United States to legalize their status and secure U.S. permanent residency and, if they desired, seek naturalization as U.S. cit-izens (see Donato 1993). Of particular relevance are the Special Agricultural Worker provisions (SAW I and II) that provided amnesty for agricultural laborers. Notably, the majority of agricultural workers (and nearly all of the individuals I interviewed) who received amnesty through IRCA were male.

The amnesty provided by IRCA was impacted by an earlier piece of legis-lation, the Immigration and Nationality Act of 1965. This legislation radically altered U.S. immigration policy by establishing family reunification—rather than national-origin quotas—as the primary criterion for immigration and naturalization. The dialectic of the Immigration and Nationality Act and IRCA has had a powerful impact on Mexican (im)migrant families: once family members were able to "legalize" their status, they could begin the process of petitioning for additional family members. The two laws operating together established a pattern of Mexican men petitioning for female spouses, children, and parents, and have routinized male-led migration and made migration a process that is inevitably linked to kin relations. The interaction of these laws and emic understandings of gender and relatedness have resulted in migrations that not only disrupt but are structured through family ties.

Current migrations from the region where I work, like previous migrations, are masculinized and primarily controlled by men: men generally go north to work and women typically migrate to reunite with family or a partner. The gendered dimensions of migrations persist even as the specifics are unstable and shifting. Migrations to the United States from other regions of Mexico also tend to be masculinized (e.g., Cohen, Rios, and Byars 2009; Cohen, Rodriguez, and Fox 2008; for the gendered aspects of internal Mexican migration, see Castellanos 2010). The autonomous movement and migration of females is much more regulated than that of males and, in general, actively discouraged. These gendered migrations result in transnational households in which men are concentrated in the United States, and women and children are in communities in Mexico.

Such transnational gendered residences illustrate how families are in flux, and point to some important changes in kinship configurations. The 1990s and the first decades of the 2000s have been characterized by transnational lives unprecedented among prior generations. According to transnational Mexicans, today's children move back and forth to a much greater extent than previous generations, typically migrating more often and for longer stays than their parents and grandparents (see chaps. 6 and 7). Initiated by immigration legislation in the 1990s and reinforced by post-9/11 U.S. practices, transnational families with members of mixed U.S. legal status living apart for years at a time have become the norm (see chaps. 3 and 7).

In large part, it is the political-economic context of the daily lives of Mexican transmigrants (e.g., Kearney 1995, 1996; Rouse 1991, 1992) that creates patterns of intimate migrations, although the actions of individuals and notions of gender and family within transnational communities are also significant. Anthropologists have drawn on social theorists from diverse fields to understand how individual agents interface with structural forces and constraints (e.g., Bourdieu 1977), focusing on the ways that agents negotiate and act within state structures and institutions. The anthropologist Sherry B. Ortner's concept of "structures of agency" (Ortner 1996: 13) productively captures the complexities of power relations between and among individuals and institutions. Informed by this notion of "embedded agency" (Ortner 1996: 13), I trace the actions of individuals, couples, and family networks against a backdrop of the U.S. state's construction of illegality. This is the complicated and shifting terrain of intimate migrations.

Ethnography in/of the Borderlands

My analysis comes out of binational, itinerant, ethnographic research among Mexican (im)migrants—women and men, girls and boys—with ties to the Mexican states of San Luis Potosí and Zacatecas and several locales in the U.S. West and Southwest. This project has been a "multi-sited ethnography . . . in/ of the world system" (Marcus 1995: 95), focused particularly on a small, agricultural town I call San Marcos in San Luis Potosí, Mexico, and in Albuquerque, New Mexico, with stays in other locations where community members live within both Mexico (several small towns surrounding San Marcos and the capital cities of San Luis Potosí and Zacatecas) and the United States (San Diego, California, and Las Vegas and Reno, Nevada). I conducted longitudinal transnational field research based in Albuquerque from 1997 through 2001 and during 2002–2003; in Mexico during 2001–2002, the summers of 2004, 2006, and 2008, and for nine months in 2010; in San Diego from 2003 to 2005; and for most of the period between 2005 and the present, in southern Nevada and, then, my current home in northern Nevada. My analysis is the result of relationships built over time and across distance. Through a focus that privileges "relations, rather than . . . locations" (Olwig and Hastrup 1997: 9), I have "follow[ed] the people" (Marcus 1995: 106) to create an ethnography of translocal family networks.

The individuals I work with are part of an extensive and not easily delineated transnational community. Therefore, ethnographic descriptions I provide about migrants are intended to capture the diversity of Mexican migrants' experiences, rather than define or demarcate a unified or homogenous community. This complex network of transnational Mexicans includes extended kin as well as friends and neighbors. The population of San Marcos fluctuates depending on the year and time of the year, ranging from approximately 250 to 350 people in recent years, with several hundred additional individuals in the United States. More than 150 members of the network are concentrated in Albuquerque, another approximately 150 are in Dallas, Texas, with additional migrants living throughout other U.S. states: primarily in the West, including California, Colorado, Nevada, Oregon, and Washington, and a few individuals and families in states in other parts of the country, such as Indiana and Delaware. Because of the frequent movement of community members between the United States and Mexico, it is difficult to provide exact figures of individuals in various locations; I offer estimates of the population recognizing that fluidity characterizes the lives of these (im)migrants.

As with transnational movement and mobility, the theme and experience of not migrating or staying is also central to my research. While the majority of people I work with are on the move and have lives that are undeniably transnational, there are others who do not migrate and may be understood as "nonmovers," "stayers" (Faist 1997b: 187), "stay at homes" (Cohen 2002), or those who are "immobile" (Hammar and Tamas 1997: 2). Increasingly, scholars recognize that the study of "immobility or non-migration" (Hammar and Tamas 1997: 17) and the inclusion of people who migrate and those who stay (Hammar et al. 1997) have much to contribute to migration studies; indeed, a look at only migrants is inadequate (Faist 1997b: 187). Researchers consider questions related to who goes, who stays, and how migrating or not affects families and communities (see Faist 1997a); aim to explain or quantify moving and staying; or look at decision-making processes (e.g., Werner and Barcus 2009). The insights from this work include a focus on the causes of immobility, such as the "confluence of economic pressures and changing border enforcement tactics" (Cornelius et al. 2010, xii; see also Hicken, Cohen, and Narvaez 2010), and expanded definitions of immobility that may include the "reduced circularity of migration flows" (Hicken, Cohen, and Narvaez 2010: 88), showing how even migrants take part in processes of immobility.

The many barriers to movement, especially those produced by the U.S. state, are a focus of the book, as are the forms of mobility that shape migrants' experiences. However, while mobility and immobility continue to shape transnational lives, it can be difficult to delineate individuals as those who are "movers" and those who are "nonmovers." While I agree about the importance of including analysis of immobility in any study of migration, I do so with the caveat that migrants and those who do not migrate are too often defined in opposition to one another, and that the many categories employed in such research—movers and nonmovers, migrants and nonmigrants, those who go and those who stay, and mobility and immobility—are in reality shifting and not easily predictable. There is fluidity in the categories themselves: for example, a "nonmover" may suddenly migrate or a "mover" may be deported and stop migrating seasonally.

Thus, I study those who move and those who do not, within both Mexico and the United States, paying particular attention to the ways in which the lives of transnational Mexicans problematize rigid categories of "mobility" and "immobility." Such (im)mobility among transnational Mexicans takes different forms. Within families, some members migrate while others do not (part I) and typically (im)mobility is gendered: men are likely to go while women tend to stay (part II). And while very young children increasingly migrate both north and south, migration is also mediated by age (part III). Structural forces, community ideals, family priorities, and individual choices come together to shape the trajectories of those who migrate and those who do not at different points in the lives of transnational Mexicans.

Recognizing that the lines that divide movement and nonmovement or migration, immigration, and immobility can be tenuous ones, and how the category of "immigrant" is "posited always from the standpoint of the migrant-receiving nation-state, in terms of outsiders coming in" (De Genova 2002: 421), I use a variety of terms interchangeably to discuss the participants in my research: "transnational Mexicans," "(im)migrants" and "(im)migration," and "transmigrant" or "transmigration" (Glick Schiller, Basch, Blanc-Szanton 1995: 48). I build on research that considers migration broadly as the movement of people from one locale to another and on scholarship that challenges the conceptualization of migration as a predictable or uniform process through the study of transnationalism (e.g., Appadurai 1996; Basch, Glick Schiller, and Szanton Blanc 1994; Glick Schiller, Basch, and Blanc-Szanton 1992; Kearney 1995, 1998; Rouse 1991, 1992; among others) and transnationality (Ong 1999). Similarly, I employ the terms "unauthorized" and "undocumented" to describe migrants who are labeled by the U.S. Department of Homeland Security and in public discourse as "illegal," recognizing that migrants are often "informally and formally authorized" to be in the United States (Plascencia 2009).

El Otro Lado/The Other Side

I first began fieldwork "at home," "*el otro lado*," in Albuquerque, New Mexico. While many anthropologists who study migration have "followed" their informants from fieldwork sites to communities in the United States and Europe, this process was reversed in my case: I met individuals in their U.S.

home, and then went to their hometowns in Mexico. My entrée into this transnational community took place in 1997 when I volunteered as an ESL and U.S. Citizenship instructor with the Albuquerque Border City Project (ABC) and an affiliated organization, Latinos Unidos. One of the few immigrant service providers in northern New Mexico at the time, ABC has since dissolved because of difficulties receiving sufficient financial support, a symptom of a political climate that has been increasingly nativist and anti-immigrant (Chavez 2008). For several years, I taught weekly classes, as well as assisted my students with the citizenship process: helping them fill out forms, translating correspondence from what was then the U.S. Immigration and Naturalization Service (INS), tutoring for citizenship exams, and—when everything went as planned—attending swearing-in ceremonies for newly naturalized U.S. citizens and celebrating when U.S. citizenship had been obtained.

My experiences working as a teacher with (im)migrants guided my theoretical interests: my project came out of my time in the classroom, the result of connecting with several migrants and becoming involved in their lives in multiple ways. It is not coincidental that this research centers on questions of family, gender, and state power. These were topics that often came up through interactions with my students, including class discussions, informal conversations, and observations of the bureaucratic processes through which migrants regularly maneuver. The difficulties faced by families living across the U.S.-Mexico border, the negotiations of individuals and families tied to two nation-states, and the gendered character of transborder movement are not abstract concepts in the lives of transnational Mexicans. Such issues are present in migrants' daily practices in concrete ways and thus became central topics of study.

Over the years, I became close with several individuals and was warmly welcomed by their extended families. By attending social events in Albuquerque—including weddings, baptisms, first communion services, and birthday and holiday parties at migrants' homes—I was introduced to a highly mobile transnational community. In New Mexico, I met individuals with divergent migration experiences, for example, community members who live part of each year in Mexico, U.S. citizens with family ties to Mexico, newcomers on their first day in the United States, as well as individuals passing through New Mexico on their way to Washington or en route to another locale from Texas. They insisted that someday I should visit them in Mexico—that I really should see their beloved *patria*—and much to their surprise, one day I actually did.

"A Very Lonely Town"

More than one thousand miles south of the U.S.-Mexico border, off the high-
way between Monterrey and Zacatecas, in the corner of the state of San Luis
Potosí, is the small rancho that I call San Marcos. San Marcos was originally
established as an *ejido*—communal agricultural plots created through land
reform after the Mexican Revolution—and its history shapes the community
today. Currently, most of San Marcos' residents are women, children, and
the elderly; the town is now less than one-third the size it was at its peak.
Because the demographics have shifted significantly over the past decades,
residents often describe San Marcos as "*un rancho muy solo*/a very lonely
town." The oldest living resident and a founding member of the community,
Don Alberto, who was in his nineties when I first interviewed him, remembers going to San Marcos with his parents and siblings after the Mexican
Revolution. Prior to establishing San Marcos with four other families, Don
Alberto's parents had worked on the *hacienda* that was then divided into *eji-
dos* throughout the region.

In San Marcos, people live in a centralized area, surrounded by family plots of land. Although pinto bean farming is the principal livelihood
in the area, the terrain is not very hospitable to agriculture. The people of
San Marcos have spent the last century working the land without irrigation,
dependent on scarce rain in Mexico's high desert. Today, the primary source
of income for most of the families in San Marcos comes from remittances
that migrants send. Virtually every family in the rancho has been touched
by migration to the United States. And, although the impact of migration
on the rancho in the past several decades has been immense, it is not the
first time residents of San Marcos have made the trip north. The fathers and
grandfathers of today's transmigrants were recruited by the U.S. government
as laborers through the Bracero Program (1942–64), traveling back and forth
between the United States and Mexico as their children and grandchildren
do today.

During life-history interviews, men from the community who worked
as braceros have recounted how migration from San Marcos to Albuquerque and Dallas established important routes or "circuits" (Rouse 1991). After
the Bracero Program ended, males from San Marcos continued to travel
to the United States as seasonal agricultural workers, contracting directly
with individual growers. Contacts made in the States eventually led them to
other work opportunities, primarily within urban areas, in construction and
other labor. Beginning in the 1970s, men from San Marcos were working in

Dallas and Albuquerque for extended periods of time, and some started to bring their spouses and children to live in Texas and New Mexico. By the late 1970s, there were several families from San Marcos living in the United States. Today, the community's ties with the United States are strong, evident in frequent movement north and south, the many community members working in *el norte*, and the ways that virtually every family is structured transnationally.

During fieldwork stays in Mexico, I lived with three families, including a family with young children; a woman who is mother, grandmother, and great-grandmother to multiple generations of migrants and whose children I first met in the United States; and a schoolteacher and her family at their residence adjacent to the school. Being part of these different households influenced and directed my research. For example, I spent many afternoons in a small store owned by one of the families who hosted me. This was a place where many men gathered to socialize, and so during my time there I talked with men and heard their stories of the past, harrowing tales of crossing the border, and descriptions of dangerous or illegal working conditions. The school, too, was a setting that provided rich ethnographic data, for it was a center of activity where parents, especially mothers, and children of all ages gathered and socialized. At the school, conversations primarily among women centered on the emotional and financial struggles of families living transnationally. When I lived with an elder in the community, family members of different ages and generations living in Mexico and the United States often visited and were in San Marcos for extended stays. These different locales and social spaces guided and facilitated the research and introduced me to people of all ages with diverse migration experiences.

Transnational Ethnography and Methods

Although I have been based in particular sites in Mexico and the United States, whenever possible I have traveled, sometimes with (im)migrants, moving transnationally between Mexico and the United States and within both countries. Within Mexico, I accompanied individuals to different locations, for example to Zacatecas to obtain a Mexican passport or to Fresnillo to pick up family members arriving from the United States by bus. During my time in Mexico, I made trips to the United States and back, including one with a family member of a former ESL student and a trip to Albuquerque for the *quinceañera* of a young migrant who had moved to the United States when she was five years old. On trips north, I often went with gifts and letters from the rancho to family and friends living in the United States. These included boxes of fresh cheese, dried chiles, just-harvested *nopalitos* [cactus], and bottles of "Mexican" Coca-Cola. On trips south, I transported gifts, television sets, clothing, and money. By moving between the two countries, I was able to gather a range of data that would not have otherwise been accessible to me.

My position as a wife and mother, a white U.S. citizen, and researcher educated in the United States both limited and facilitated access to particular individuals and topics. For example, I had varying access to men and women; it was much easier for me to visit and talk with women than it was to do so with men. Not only was it culturally acceptable to visit more often and converse more intimately with women, there were cultural practices already in place that enabled me to do so. Among migrants I know, there is a distinct gender division—in work, social settings, religious practice, and family roles. Men spend much of their time with other men, and women are frequently with other women and children. Certainly, the interactions I have had with women and mothers have been among the most personal and candid. Despite differences in positionality, though, over the years I have conducted fieldwork with diverse individuals in terms of gender, family position, age, immigration status, and geographic location.

One research exchange that was mediated by positionality and especially gender, for example, was when I visited a family without realizing that the *señora* of the house was spending the day in a nearby town. Her husband, Ricardo, a migrant whom I had met on prior occasions, answered the door and explained that his wife was away. Ricardo asked me about my research and spoke with me for nearly an hour about his migrations to the United States. However, he never invited me into his home (as women always did)—instead, we had an hour-long conversation standing at the doorway. It would not have been appropriate for me to enter the house, especially since neither Ricardo's wife nor my husband was there with us. Nevertheless, the man openly shared his experiences about life in the United States as we spoke. Many of my interactions with men were in public places or mixed company, such as during a meal or at events when family members and friends came together. Because I taught English classes, I also had the opportunity to interact with boys and men in a classroom setting, in both Mexico and the United States.

Recognizing the role of the anthropologist as "instrument of observation" (Kearney 2004: 2) and employing different methodologies have enabled me to integrate rich and varied data. Over the course of the research I conducted interviews and oral histories, carried out extensive participant observation, employed visual methods such as photography and videography to collect data and document transnational relationships, and engaged in public anthropology (e.g., Farmer 2004; Nordstrom 2004; Ong 2003), especially through work with community organizations. I also used ethnographic questionnaires to guide interviews and trace family genealogies. The body of the study included interviews and participant observation. I formally and informally interviewed more than 160 people for the project—the majority were adults and children who participated in ongoing research over the years and were interviewed several times. I have also had brief conversations with many other individuals at marketplaces, during family events, or traveling to different places in Mexico.

The ethnographic interviews were structured and open-ended, brief and lengthy, recorded and not recorded. Conversations as someone fed pigs, on a bumpy ride to Zacatecas, or at a home in Albuquerque provided some of the richest data I collected. I conducted interviews and gathered life history narratives in both Mexico and the United States, in Spanish and/or English, depending on the preference of the interviewee. I spoke with individuals of all ages—from preschool students to the eldest members of the community—and with varied (im)migration histories. Interviews with elders often became oral histories with a focus on the past and change over time, while exchanges with young children emphasized the present and future. I interviewed men and women, boys and girls, people who were single, married, divorced, and widowed. Whenever possible, I conducted follow-up interviews and interviewed individuals in multiple settings—for example, I visited with multiple (im)migrants at their home in Albuquerque and later, in their *casa* in the rancho, or met individuals in Mexico and then saw them again, or met their family members, in the United States.

Systematic participant observation was also central to this project. I analyzed activities and events in both Mexico and the United States, which ranged from making tortillas to elaborate family celebrations. As is the strength of ethnographic research, interviews and observations overlapped, and were conducted over an extended period of time. For example, Lucía (Introduction and chap. 2) was a student of mine in Albuquerque in 1997—I interviewed her multiple times, attended many of her family gatherings, and most recently we visited in San Marcos during the summer of 2010. I first met Rosa (chap. 4) when I was in Mexico in 2001–2002. During that year I interviewed her and visited her home on several occasions, and socialized with her and other women at the school. When I returned to the United States in 2002, I met her husband

and sons, who were living in Albuquerque, and interviewed them. Each time I was in Mexico (2004, 2006, 2008, and 2010), I again interviewed Rosa. I also have had a long-term friendship with José and his family (chap. 5). Over the years, we have had countless conversations, recorded a formal interview, and traveled together to visit his parents and siblings in another rancho on several occasions (2001, 2004, 2008, 2010). Ofelia (Introduction and Conclusion) traveled with us to the United States and, during twenty-five hours we were in the car together, recounted many events throughout her lifetime. I interviewed her multiple times over the past decade. These cases demonstrate the importance of combining interviews and participant observation, and the value of using these methods in tandem.

I realized early on that formal, structured interviews were not always the most effective way to collect data for the project, especially given the topics I studied. For example, during one recorded interview with a woman in Mexico, I asked her to describe an "ideal man." She paused for a minute, and then said she really could not answer the question, that in fact no man is ideal. However, just minutes after we ended the interview and I turned off the recorder, she spoke with me informally as she began preparing dinner for her family. She described the qualities of a "good man"—devotion to family, one who migrates to provide financially, a man who puts his children first. Many social exchanges that took place in families' homes contributed to the book, and observations were particularly useful in building my analyses about gender (part II). Still, while informal exchanges were often among the most revealing, there were topics that I was able to explore through more structured methods. For example, I traced families and family genealogies utilizing kinship charts and ethnographic questionnaires. The kinship charts provided visual representations of families, and using an ethnographic questionnaire as a guide to conversations, I was able to gather migration histories and the geographic locations of individuals in a consistent way across families.

I went into the field with two invaluable research tools: a digital video camera and a digital 35-mm camera. The photographs and video footage that I gathered have provided visual fieldnotes from my years of research, and I consider these to be as central to my analysis and findings as text-based data and notes. I took and distributed "transnational" photographs: with my digital camera, I photographed individuals on both sides of the border, then printed photos and delivered them to family on the other side. On numerous occasions, individuals asked me to take particular photographs of family members or to videotape an event using my camera and/or their own video camera; their "view" of important images to document provided significant data. And in recent years, several families have asked me to take photographs of existing prints of family photographs and then create enlarged copies. These diverse photos and videotapes are data that have contributed directly to this work for what they reveal about constructing family across the U.S.-Mexico border, as well as the ties and divisions that transnational families experience.

Disposable cameras served as another visual methodological strategy. I distributed the cameras to individuals—children and adults—with family members in the United States. They took photographs that they wished to send to family members in the north, typically of themselves, their houses, and their farms and animals. I had the images developed in Mexico, gave copies to research participants, talked with them about the photographs they took and why they were meaningful, and then took a set to family members in the United States. In addition, I gave disposable cameras to youth to photograph their schools, friends, and daily activities. These photos especially informed my arguments about youth's gender performances (see chap. 6).

Visual methodologies were ways to elicit alternative perspectives, especially among young people including very young children. Working with teachers at the preschool, elementary school, and middle school, I organized a series of art projects in the rancho. Students painted pieces depicting their transnational families and their ideas about Mexico and the United States. While they painted, I photographed children with their artwork and talked with them about the impact of migration in the rancho and their experiences with transnational migration. The art projects provided data for parts I and III of the book. Overall, such visual methodological strategies augmented interviews and participant observation, capturing thoughts and feelings of transnational Mexicans that may not have been expressed in the context of more typical methodologies.

Over the course of my research, then, I have employed diverse and intersecting methodological strategies. In the study of the intimate spheres of family and gender, ethnographic research is one of the few ways to explicate subjectivities along lines of gender, family position, and age, and to understand nuanced interactions within families. It has also been a rigorous way to consider migrants' perspectives of state action, providing a telling view of state power within migrants' lives. I have used these many exchanges—observations of everyday life—to guide my research. This is the work of ethnography, and I hope the richness of incorporating diverse methods comes through in the data presented here.

Mapping the Book

Recognizing the interconnectedness of multiple dichotomies, I have structured my analysis in a way that captures this complexity. The book is organized around three central and overlapping themes: family across the U.S.-Mexico border, gendered selves and relations, and childhood and migration. Each part includes a chapter focused on migrants' understandings of gender and kin followed by a chapter that demonstrates the ways the U.S. categorization of (im)migrants as "legal" or "illegal" penetrates intimate lives.

Part I examines the ways that family relations impact and are influenced by the migratory process and state regimes. Binational families are the subject of chapter 2. The chapter explores the effect of transnational movement on gendered kin relations and examines the ways that families living across an international border are both divided and united transnationally. Chapter 3 focuses on a defining element of current U.S. immigration policy—family reunification—to consider how the construction of (il)legality results in shifting configurations of kinship in a transnational space. A focus on individuals as embedded within families problematizes popular conceptions of migrants as solely autonomous agents, uncovering the multiple ways in which the actions of family members are repeatedly shaped and constrained by state policies.

Part II further develops my analysis of gender, a theme that runs throughout the book. Chapter 4 looks at how (im)migration directs and impacts gender relations and subjectivities, and outlines the changing roles of women and men. Chapter 5 considers the complexities of gender and power in the context of the U.S. state. Gendered crossings illustrate how unauthorized entry and migration, as well as the perils of unauthorized movement, are shaped by one's gender in shifting circumstances. The chapter also focuses on what I consider to be the "gendered transgressions" of transnationality, demonstrating how the state's presence and the specter of "illegality" (re)configure desire, infidelity, and gendered violence.

Part III turns to the next generation to examine the ways that migrations connect to children of all ages, from infants to young people embarking on adulthood. Chapter 6 examines children who migrate and those who do not. The recognition of children as principal actors, and the inclusion of young people as fundamentally central to migration, contributes to broader understandings of migrant agency—and its limitations—along lines of age, gender, and generation. Chapter 7 again turns to categorization by the U.S. state, this time emphasizing how U.S. immigration policies and practices create a form of contingent citizenship, a concept that—while applicable to all transnational Mexicans—is particularly evident among the youngest of migrants, those with or without documents.

The book's conclusion revisits how migrants operate both within and outside of nation-states. The experience of being *between here and there* is increasingly defined by exclusion. Although individuals and families do, at times, act outside of state control, circumventing the state and/or strategically using state policies and practices as they are able, the U.S. state has far-reaching effects in transnational Mexicans' everyday lives. The postscript considers how growing anti-immigrant sentiment in the United States is likely to affect intimate lives in emergent, and troubling, ways.

PART I

Transborder Families

Mitad Allá, Mitad Aquí/
Half There, Half Here

In an interview at the dining room table of her Albuquerque home, a former ESL and U.S. citizenship student, Lucía (see Introduction)—articulated the experience of being part of a transnational family. "I think that I am divided," she explained. "I consider Mexico my home, but I think of my home as [the United States] because here I have had many opportunities and this is where I live. So I am confused when I think about home . . . I think of home as half there, half here [*mitad allá, mitad aquí*] . . . half in Mexico and half here." A few weeks after I interviewed Lucía, I visited with her at a party held in honor of her daughter and niece on the day of their first communion. Lucía talked with different family members—her father-in-law who was in town for a one-month visit, her brother who lived a few blocks away, her teenage daughter who had just started taking classes at the community college. Lucía later told me that she was disappointed that her family living in Mexico could not be part of the celebration. She said that at holidays and family parties, she feels especially nostalgic about the rancho. "I know it is not possible, but sometimes I wish that we could all live in one place."

Individuals, couples, and families living across an international border experience the contradictory processes of continuity and fragmentation. Even as the U.S.-Mexico border divides couples and families, Mexican (im)migrants build relationships and construct home and family in a manner that transcends nation-states. Despite the fluid movement of transnational Mexicans between the United States and Mexico, the border is a barrier with a powerful and far-reaching impact on families and the geographic and symbolic locations of kin. Ultimately, for Mexican (im)migrants, constructing home, marriage, and family is a transnational endeavor, one that bridges—yet is always ruptured by—the U.S.-Mexico border.

Families in Flux

Laura and Federico González have been married for more than twenty years; they have six children, ranging in age from three to nineteen years old. In some ways, the González family has a life quite typical of many Mexicans, as well as many families living in the United States: Federico and his two eldest sons work to support the family; Laura manages their home, prepares meals, and is the primary caregiver for the children; and the four youngest González children attend school full time. But the González family is distinct as well. They do not live together, in fact, they live more than one thousand miles apart, and they have not been all in one place for more than three years. The experiences of this transnational family, like those of the extended families described in the following section, demonstrate how kinship transcends and challenges nation-state boundaries. The daily lives of the González family also emphasize the difficulties of living in multiple nations, and illustrate how familial and marital ties are more often than not, severed by the U.S.-Mexico border.

The experiences of the González family highlight many of the kinship transformations underway among Mexican (im)migrants and point to some of the changes discussed in this chapter and throughout the book. The González family lives in a gendered transnational household: Federico and two sons live in an Albuquerque apartment with other males from San Marcos, while Laura and the four youngest González children live in the rancho. Laura and Federico have experienced strains living so many years apart—there have been allegations that Federico was in an extramarital relationship—yet they are committed to sustaining their transnational family. Finally, migration is prominent in the lives of their children: two González sons left for Albuquerque with their father when they were fifteen and sixteen years old, and another son, who is fourteen, is considering when it will be best to join his family in the United States. The youngest González, at age three, has never met his father and eldest brothers. Although they are undocumented, Laura and Federico hope to reunite their family in Albuquerque within a few years, and they are saving money to cover the cost of *coyote/as* to relocate five family members (a *coyote/a* is man or woman who facilitates entry into the United States). These are the cross-border links as well as the prominent divisions that are part of the daily lives of the González family.

Kinship ties are inextricably intertwined with transnational movement, and family and marriage more often than not guide migration. "Transnational kinship" (Glick Schiller and Fouron 2001) and "transnational families" (Chavez 1992: 121) are a reality for migrants: every family in the rancho is structured through transnational ties, even in cases when most members are living in Mexico or in the United States. Partners, children, and siblings, as well as extended family members, live on both sides of the border—indeed, "the fates of family and nation are directly and intimately related" (Glick Schiller and Fouron 2001: 60). As the anthropologist Roger Rouse has argued, such families live in an "alternative cartography of social space" (Rouse 1991: 12), finding "that their most important kin and friends are as likely to be living hundreds or thousands of miles away as immediately around them" (Rouse 1991: 13). For transmigrant communities, family is configured, defined, and "scattered" (Coe 2008: 237) within a transnational space and, significantly, separated by an international boundary and severed because of the policies of and relations between nation-states.

In a transnational context, "family" may include partners, parents, children, siblings, grandparents and grandchildren, (great) aunts/uncles and (grand) nieces/nephews, cousins, *compadres* and *comadres*, and godparents and godchildren, among others. These multiple family relations support migration: relationships with relatives profoundly influence migration trajectories. In fact, migrations are never entirely autonomous or disconnected from family. Migrants typically cross with family members, and when they do not, their migrations are linked to kin in other substantive ways—people migrate to support family, to reunite with family, and/or with financial and social resources from family members. There are also many conflicts at this nexus of family and migration; transnational movement often creates and/or is the result of disputes and hardship within and between families.

The notion of family is, in any setting, characterized by fluidity and diversity. Despite a tendency in the social sciences to reify family and "treat it as an entity or 'black box' rather than a collection of people and relationships" (Creed 2000), anthropologists have a long tradition of uncovering the variability that characterizes kin throughout the world. Feminists have challenged scholars to complicate often naturalized kinship categories, questioning the notion of an always cohesive "household" (e.g., Bjerén 1997) and problematizing "family" itself (Collier, Rosaldo, and Yanagisako 1997; Collier and Yanagisako 1987; Ginsburg and Tsing 1990; Lamphere, Ragoné, and Zavella 1997; Thorne and Yalom 1992). Transnational families are, without question, dynamic. Migrants, whose lives are characterized by frequent movement, continuously maintain, reassert, reconfigure, and transform family (Cole and Durham 2007; Glick Schiller and Fouron 2001; Olwig 2007; Olwig and Hastrup 1997). The meanings and significance attached to particular family relations are never fixed and notably malleable in the context of transnational migration. Migration is accelerating the process of change within families, or perhaps, bringing transformations in family ties and kinship structures into clearer view.

Borderland Families

Kinship formations are not and have never been static, and there are multiple ways that migrants structure their lives and homes. Beginning in the 1970s, and accelerating in the 1980s through the present, transnationality and families that extend across the U.S.-Mexico border have become increasingly prominent in migrants' lives. As discussed, men first migrated as braceros in the 1940s, contracting with the U.S. state to provide agricultural labor. Significantly, during the Bracero Program males migrated alone, returning seasonally and maintaining lives and families that were firmly rooted in Mexico. It was not until the 1970s and 1980s that families began migrating together to the United States, and even today, it is not typical. A pattern of male-led migration that takes place in stages—men are concentrated in United States, and women and children live in the rancho with families reuniting after years apart—persists, albeit unevenly, demonstrating how the Bracero Program has shaped contemporary transnational family structures.

This section focuses on three family networks—a family living primarily in the rancho, a network divided between the two countries, and a family with most members in New Mexico—to introduce the range of migration experiences, residential arrangements, gendered politics, and likely future trajectories among transnational Mexicans living in the extended U.S.-Mexico borderlands. The transnational lives of these community members illustrate patterns in locating family across the border as well as underscore the diverse ways that transmigrants move—or do not migrate—between Mexico and the United States. These distinct family trajectories also demonstrate the gendered dimensions of familial ties: in general, migrations depend on males to facilitate movement, and families with male relatives living in the United States are better positioned to migrate. As the experiences of the families underscore, networks with well-established male migration patterns are likely to have multiple family members living in the United States, while families without such circuits find migration to be much more difficult.

Finally, the diverse paths of these families illustrate the difficulties in assuming a common history or predictable course in migration flows and family structures. While it may seem likely that a family with most members in Mexico is in the process of moving toward eventual reunification in the United States, such futures are never certain. It is increasingly difficult to bring together family in *el norte* in ways that families did in the late 1980s and 1990s. In the twenty-first century and especially post 9/11, as stays in the United States have become longer and passage back and forth more complicated, reuniting family is an increasingly challenging endeavor.

La Familia Luna

The majority of members of the Luna family live in Mexico. Although several families in the rancho are part of established transnational networks, the Luna family has limited ties to the United States. Four of the five Luna siblings, Delfina, Berta, Carmela, and Domingo, currently live in Mexico— three in San Marcos, one in a neighboring town—and only one of the Luna siblings, Sara, who currently lives in Atlanta, has ever migrated to the United States. Families such as the Lunas are the exception. Typically, such families would like to have members migrate but are unable to do so because of few resources—financial as well as support from migrants—available to them.

One of the Luna sisters, Carmela, has frequently told me that she would like her husband and children to go to the United States to work. One morning, Carmela's youngest daughter came to the house where I was staying, and relayed a message from her mother—could I please visit her mother as soon as possible? She needed to talk with me. It was important and, in fact, somewhat urgent. I left immediately and entered the family's small *tienda*.

"*Venga,*" Carmela said as she gestured for me to come inside. She was whispering and looked concerned. "We need your help with the consulate. They denied our visas again." She pulled out a small stack of papers. "What can you do to help us?" she asked. I looked at the letter on top. It said that family members had been denied a tourist visa and that they would have to wait at least one year before applying again. I tried to explain that there was little I could do, that unfortunately I did not have any influence with the U.S. consulate, but Carmela was persistent—she told me that she hoped to visit her sister, Sara, who was living in Georgia with her boyfriend. "Come, let's visit my parents to discuss this."

I followed Carmela into a small *jardin*, repeating my lack of power in matters with the U.S. government. Carmela just waved at me to stop talking. We walked down one of the principal streets in San Marcos, a dirt road slightly wider than the rest, and entered her parents' compound. Carmela's mother, Dolores, was working in the kitchen. As always, Dolores warmly welcomed me, holding my hands and smiling. "Debbie, what a nice surprise. It has been so long since your last visit," she said, although I had come by her house just a week earlier. Carmela's father, Bruno, stood from his meal at the dining room table and shook my hand. He said that he had spent the day in the fields, "With this heat, it is uncertain when the rain will come."

Dolores directed us into a sitting room filled with cages and dozens of brightly colored birds. Her two small grandchildren, Noemi and Efrán said "*hola*," and then ran outside to play. As she took off her apron and brushed hair away from her face, Dolores told me she was very tired—caring for Sara's children while she was in Atlanta was exhausting, although, she insisted, she wouldn't trade the opportunity for anything. In fact, she said, she feared the day when Sara would send for Noemi and Efrán, and then she would have to face the possibility of not seeing them for years, or even worse, dying before they returned to the rancho again. "Wouldn't it be wonderful if Carmela and her family were able to obtain visas and visit Sara?" she asked suddenly. I repeated that I wished I could help but that I really had no influence with agents at the U.S. consulate. "Could you telephone them and explain our situation? Wouldn't they listen to you, a *profesora*?" After lengthy discussion, we agreed that I would call the consulate and try to set up another appointment.

Because the Luna family does not have established ties in the United States, they live on the margins of San Marcos' transnational community. It is telling that the only sibling to migrate is female; within families with many transmigrants, migrations are almost without exception male-led. The majority of single females who go to the United States from San Marcos do so under the same conditions that Sara did—faced with the need to support her children, Sara had few options. Even Sara's migration, however, depended on male support. Ultimately, she was able to go to the United States with the help of a new boyfriend, Leonardo. She met Leonardo at a dance in a neighboring rancho, and within a few months, the couple left for Georgia, where several of Leonardo's brothers and extended family were living. By joining an established migration circuit, Sara was able to go north to work and send money home for her two children.

I had the chance to talk with Sara several times by telephone. "I miss my children desperately!" she told me one evening. "I plan to bring them soon, although I know it will be very difficult for my mother." Sara said that she hoped to have a relative of her boyfriend cross with them and bring them to Atlanta to be reunited with her. She said that when her children would make the trip north was uncertain, but that she was working long hours at a fast-food restaurant to earn extra money to pay for their passage. Sara's relatives in Mexico hope to travel to the United States, although doing so would require migrating with the help of Sara's boyfriend's family network. This tenuous connection to the United States means that it will be difficult for other members of the Luna family to migrate in the near future. In the short term, it is likely that the majority of the Luna siblings will stay in Mexico, but continue to strategize about possible routes to the United States.

La Familia Salazar

The Salazar family lives divided by the border: this family is, quite literally, split down the middle, with about half of the family living in the United States and the other half in Mexico. This family network is geographically divided in specifically gendered ways. The three Salazar brothers and their eldest male sons currently live in Albuquerque, while their wives and younger children remain in San Marcos. The Salazar family's migrations are relatively recent. Rolando and Sergio, two Salazar brothers who are both in their forties, left for New Mexico in 1999, crossing the border with a *coyote* at Ciudad Juárez–El Paso. They had the support of several cousins and an uncle, who hosted them in their home and helped them secure work with a construction company. After ten months, Rolando and Sergio moved into an apartment together and asked their brother Teodoro and two of Rolando's sons to join them. Teodoro and his nephews made the trip north and crossed together, also with the assistance of a *coyote*.

Meanwhile, the wives of the Salazar brothers, Ramona (married to Sergio), Soledad (married to Rolando), and Conzuela (married to Teodoro), stayed in San Marcos. One afternoon, I visited with Soledad in her small family home. The house was modest, even by local standards, with four rooms—a living room, kitchen, and two bedrooms. The family had not yet been able to afford a bathroom, but Soledad said she was hopeful that with her husband's and sons' wages they would be able to build one soon.

Soledad described to me what a typical day is like for her, now that her husband is gone. "I'm so busy!" she exclaimed. "I was busy before, but now I work around the clock." She recounted how she accompanies the four children who live with her off to school, then she feeds the animals and begins cooking. Mid-morning she takes a meal to the children during their break from classes, and returns to mop the house and sweep the patio before school lets out. The afternoon is dedicated to serving the largest meal of the day, *comida*, filling the household's large tubs with water, washing dishes, and doing the family's laundry. After lunch, she runs errands—going to a nearby rancho to make calls from her sister's telephone, stopping by a neighbor's house to pick up her daughter's school uniform, or driving out to the *milpas* to check on the hired farmhand's progress. As I listened to her talk about her daily activities, Soledad took out a small photograph in a rusted frame. The photo was of a thin man with a large mustache and a serious expression. There was an inscription across the back of the photo where Rolando had written, "*A mi querida Soledad, te amo* [For my dear Soledad, I love you]." "I miss him so," she said. "And my sons as well. Hopefully we can all be together soon. It has already been several years."

Months later, I visited the Salazar men one evening in their Albuquerque apartment. I was delivering a letter from Soledad and picking up a package to take back to the rancho. Rolando greeted me and awkwardly invited me to have a seat on one of two folding chairs in the barren living room. The only other object in the room was a stereo sitting in a corner on the floor. Teodoro and Rolando's son were also home. Sergio and another of Rolando's sons, they explained, were working at the restaurant-bar where several of the Salazar men were currently employed. Nicolas, Rolando's seventeen-year-old nephew and the son of a Salazar sister living in the rancho, was also at the apartment. He had arrived a few months earlier. Nicolas said that he felt nostalgic about San Marcos and missed his family. He asked me to visit his parents and siblings when I returned to the rancho, and to please tell his mother that he was safe and healthy, "*gracias a diós*."

Rolando and Teodoro told me that they both hoped to bring their wives and children to Albuquerque sometime in the future. "It is very difficult to have family so far away," Teodoro told me. "I'm not sure I want my family to live here, but I don't know when I will be able to go back. Perhaps the next time you visit, my family will be here with me." Indeed, when I was back in New Mexico a year later, Teodoro had brought his family to Albuquerque, and Rolando was still considering the possibility of having his wife and children make the trip north. As the Salazar males establish deeper connections to Albuquerque, it is likely that they will try to have their female partners and younger children join them in the United States.

La Familia Moreno

The Moreno family has an established history of migration to New Mexico. Today, six of seven adult siblings are living in Albuquerque, while just one brother, Daniel, lives in Mexico in a house adjacent to his parents. Their father traveled to Texas and California as a bracero through the early 1960s, although he chose not to settle, and when the Bracero Program ended, he returned to San Marcos to farm. The first Moreno sibling to migrate was Felipe, nearly twenty years ago. Felipe helped set up a network of resources and support that has facilitated the migrations of his siblings. In addition, several of the Moreno siblings have married U.S. permanent residents and U.S. citizens, which has also assisted in establishing migration patterns among this family.

Felipe told me his story from his home in Albuquerque's Southwest Mesa. First, he took me on a tour of his newly built house—Felipe had done most of the work himself, and he was very proud of his new home. In the backyard was a mobile home, where Felipe and his family had lived during construction of the house. Felipe said that two of his cousins were currently living there.

Felipe explained that, when he first came to New Mexico, his future seemed grim. Although, he admitted, everything had turned out well for him—much better than he could have imagined. Felipe said that in the early 1980s, he was living in the rancho. He worked briefly at a gas station in a town an hour from his home, but he was not making enough money to support himself and contribute to household expenses for his extended family. In the mid-1980s, he decided to make the trip north. He crossed for the first time with a cousin and a friend, both from San Marcos. They went to Albuquerque because an uncle was living there with his family; the uncle had facilitated their migration and offered a home for their first months in the United States. Felipe went to work at a Mexican restaurant where several other residents of San Marcos were working. He spent two years in Albuquerque and met a native New Mexican, Amanda. After dating for several months, Felipe and Amanda decided to marry. Felipe became a U.S. permanent resident, and immediately began the process of petitioning for family members in Mexico.

Felipe encouraged his brothers to join him in Albuquerque, and three years after Felipe had departed, Hugo and Pascual left San Marcos for New Mexico as well. They lived temporarily with Felipe and Amanda in a mobile home, and Felipe helped them secure jobs busing tables at the Mexican restaurant where he continues to be employed, now as a food preparer. Pascual also met a U.S. citizen and married—and changed his status to U.S. permanent resident—while Hugo dated and eventually married another migrant, Paola, from a town close to San Marcos. Hugo and Paola, both undocumented, continued to live with Felipe and Amanda, while Pascual moved into a condominium with his wife.

Meanwhile, the Moreno sisters, Reina, Patricia, and Nadia, and Daniel, the other brother, were living in the rancho. Reina was married with three small children, and her husband, Moisés, was working in construction in San Jose, California. Moisés rarely sent money, and then stopped sending support altogether. Rumors in San Marcos spread—Moisés had met another woman and did not intend to financially support his wife and children. Reina felt she had no choice but to go to the United States and work. One fall, when Felipe and Amanda were visiting San Marcos for the town *fiesta*, Reina discussed her plans with them, and they agreed to assist her migration. Felipe contacted a *coyota* that he knew, and after leaving her children with her parents, Reina left for New Mexico. Once there, she, too, lived with Felipe and Amanda and began working for a clothing manufacturer, a job she secured through a friend of Amanda. She eventually met and married a migrant from San Luis Potosí, Octavio. Since Octavio had obtained U.S. permanent residency and citizenship through IRCA, Reina was able to become a U.S. permanent resident and thus bring her children to the United States.

Patricia and Nadia married men from ranchos near San Marcos, and for several years they lived with their husbands' families while their husbands farmed and they worked as homemakers. Money was very tight for these families, and the remittances sent by their brothers were irregular and not enough to live on. Felipe, Hugo, and Pascual sent money whenever they could, although their first responsibility was supporting their parents and purchasing supplies for the family farm. Over several months, the Moreno brothers living in the United States discussed the possibility of having their brothers-in-law—their sisters' husbands—migrate as well. They encouraged them to do so and offered a place to live and help securing a job. Both men, Roberto and Vidal, agreed to migrate, though Roberto decided that his wife, Patricia, and four children should stay behind; Vidal chose to migrate with his wife, Nadia, and their children. Vidal's decision was not a typical one and turned out to be quite expensive because a *coyota* was hired to cross Nadia and three children. After two years, Roberto arranged for his wife, Patricia, and children to be reunited with him and Patricia's siblings in Albuquerque. After several years in New Mexico, Vidal and Nadia divorced, and Nadia remarried, to a Mexican national who had naturalized as a U.S. citizen.

Only one of the Moreno siblings, Daniel, has yet to migrate to New Mexico. I often visited with Daniel and his family in the compound where they live with the Morenos' parents. Daniel's home in San Marcos is quite different from the home of his brother Felipe in Albuquerque. Daniel's home is built on the corner of his parents' plot of land, and it has three rooms in a row, with no bathroom and just one bedroom for this family of five. Because all of his siblings, and especially his brothers, are currently living in Albuquerque, he feels responsible for his parents and the family's land; it seems unlikely that Daniel will migrate in the near future. Felipe has petitioned for his parents, although they have expressed their desire to stay in Mexico. They hope that U.S. permanent residency will facilitate their travels to New Mexico, but they prefer to maintain their home in San Marcos.

Today, six of the seven Moreno siblings are living in the United States, with different legal statuses: Felipe and Pascual are U.S. citizens, Reina and Nadia are U.S. permanent residents, and Hugo and Patricia are undocumented. Their children also represent diverse legal positions—some are undocumented, others are U.S. permanent residents or naturalized U.S. citizens, and many were born in the United States. The Moreno family has strong ties to the United States, and because of a well-established network made up of immediate and extended kin, siblings have been able to support one another's migrations—transnational movement that has been male-led but has included males and females of all ages.

Gendered Kin Relations and Residences

These three families have experienced transnationality in different ways and to varying degrees; each family is structured and geographically situated according to access to resources, the U.S. immigration status of individuals, age, and gender. Gender intersects with notions of relatedness, U.S. immigration status, and age/generation in important ways. While later chapters explore the gendered dimensions of migration to consider shifting gender subjectivities (chap. 4), the ways that gender guides border crossings and transnational partnerships (chap. 5), and the gendered aspects of adolescents' passage to adulthood (chap. 6), the focus here is place of residence and how one's location in the transnation is shaped by but can also influence notions of gender.

Transnational migration has resulted in kinship groupings and residential patterns that are specifically gendered: predominantly male households in the United States and largely female households in Mexico are common. Because males are more likely to migrate than females, the demographic makeup of San Marcos and neighboring towns is a female majority, what locals call "*un rancho de puras mujeres*/a town of all [or only] women." Households in San Marcos are made up of primarily female adults—grandmothers, mothers, mothers-in-law, and daughters-in-law—and children of both sexes. On the other side of the border, in the United States, there are many apartments with only male residents—fathers and sons, brothers, uncles, nephews, and cousins living together in relatively close quarters. Migration, then, recasts the notion of a household, such as the case of the Salazar family. In these transnational kin groupings, migrants living thousands of miles away are understood to be part of one "household" or family unit, even as transnational residences reshape kinship patterns within both Mexico and the United States.

Gendered migrations and residences are having a profound effect on gender subjectivities and relations. In addition, such living arrangements are having a notable impact on kinship formations. Through most of the twentieth century, families in the region were patrilocal: sons and daughters-in-law built homes on or adjacent to the extended family compound, and daughters moved to the homes of their husband's family. Patrilocality was a reflection of meaningful family relations—that is, kinship as traced from fathers to sons—and served to solidify the importance of the co-residence of sons' families. This desire or ideal to maintain close geographic proximity of kin—albeit in new gendered forms—continues to define family structures in the U.S.-Mexico transnation. Today, for example, mothers-in-law and daughters-in-law often live under one roof without their husbands, which can intensify already contentious in-law relationships and create emergent kinship ties and divisions. Transnational gendered residences illustrate how families are in flux, and point to some notable changes in kinship configurations and relations between and among males and females.

Consider the experiences of Fátima and Juan Carlos. Just weeks after Fátima and Juan Carlos were married, Juan Carlos left with his father for the United States. Juan Carlos lived in Dallas, Texas, in an apartment with seven other men from San Marcos, including his father and brother, his uncle and two cousins, and two neighbors. The men cooked for themselves and one another, and took turns cleaning their barren apartment. Juan Carlos came to depend on male relatives in new ways in the United States, especially because migrants rarely live with cousins and friends in the rancho. Juan Carlos told me that it was challenging to live in Dallas with only men. He said that he did not like to cook and could not do it well, and that he missed his mother's *chile* dishes. He said that whenever he had the opportunity, he would go to his cousin's house for meals—although he knew her cooking would never measure up to that of his mother, it was better than anything he or his housemates could prepare. Juan Carlos said that he longed for *comida* at his home in the rancho, or at least, some of his mother's *salsa*. "I even have dreams that I am in the rancho eating! Yes, I miss the rancho very much."

While Juan Carlos was in Texas, Fátima was living in San Marcos with her mother-in-law, Carmen. After four years together, the two women developed a very close relationship—in fact, Fátima's mother-in-law was more like her partner in terms of her day-to-day life. Both women told me that they had a strong relationship, and that they depended on one another. They divided household chores, cared for Fátima and Juan Carlos' three-year-old daughter, and often traveled to Mexico City to visit Carmen's daughter. From my interactions with them, they seemed to genuinely enjoy one another's company without the conflict and contention that many mothers-in-law and daughters-in-law in patrilíneal communities experience. However, at the end of my field research in Mexico, Carmen and Fátima's relationship had changed significantly.

Fátima learned that her husband, Carmen's son, was with another woman in the United States. It was an extremely stressful time for both women. Fátima spent days alone in her bedroom, crying inconsolably. Carmen, whose husband had been unfaithful to her several years earlier, had a pragmatic view of the situation. "It is often unavoidable," she told me. "Infidelity doesn't mean that Juan Carlos doesn't love Fátima. After all, he married her, not another woman. Fátima is young and idealistic—it is hard for her to accept that her husband is with someone else." Carmen explained that infidelity is common among migrants: "So many years apart . . . it is very difficult for couples. As long as he continues to send money, it will be fine." Women often expressed this sentiment about men's disloyalty; chapter 5 further explores women's perspectives on the transgressions and infidelities that occur within transnational partnerships.

The infidelity was not acceptable to Fátima, however. A week after receiving the news of Juan Carlos, she took her young daughter and went back to her parents' home in a nearby rancho. In a twist that reflects how kinship is changing with migration, Fátima divorced her husband—and essentially her mother-in-law—by moving out of her mother-in-law's house, severing ties with her husband but especially with her mother-in-law. Carmen was devastated when Fátima and her granddaughter left, but Carmen felt she had no option but to support her son. Although migration and the absence of men enabled these two women to build unusually strong kinship ties, in the face of a crisis, established family loyalties, especially support of sons, prevailed. The experience of Fátima and Juan Carlos is an example of emergent manifestations of "family" in a transnational space, and of how particular relationships—such as between partners, a mother-in-law and a daughter-in law, and extended male kin—are taking on new importance and/or being undermined.

Another change in kinship arrangements is how families are structured (or not) around their farms. Patrilocality in many parts of rural Mexico has been linked to land inheritance and the day-to-day maintenance of farms. Males, based on birth order, have typically been the first in line to inherit family land, but migration is reshaping—albeit slowly—these intersecting economic and familial systems. Because of migration, males are much less likely than they were thirty years ago to live in their family's compound and to work consistently on the farm. While some males do travel seasonally from the United States to plant and harvest beans, the current political climate in the United States means that the assurance of male labor throughout the agricultural cycle in Mexico is more tenuous than in previous decades.

Given the migration of males, families employ various strategies to keep up their farms. For example, Eloy is the patriarch of a large family in which, like the Morenos, most of the adult children have migrated. All of Eloy's sons are living in the United States—three in Albuquerque and one in Dallas. Because Eloy is in his late sixties, working in the fields has become difficult for him. He explained that he gets tired after a short period of time, and Eloy's wife told me that she is worried about her husband's health. Because Eloy's sons are undocumented, they are not able to return to Mexico often, but they all send money regularly. Eloy uses these remittances to hire farmhands—his son-in-law, several nephews, and some local teens—to work in the family's fields. In addition, female family members, including two of Eloy's daughters, work in the *milpas* during particular times in the agricultural cycle, especially at harvest time. Throughout the year, women are expected to prepare food and deliver it to men while they are working in the fields, but they also join men to plant and harvest.

Although most sons migrate and spend years away from their communities, land continues to be controlled by males, and all but a handful of the approximately eighty *ejidatarios* [common land guardians] in San Marcos are men. Even when men have spent many years or decades in the United States, they continue in their role as *ejidatarios* rather than having the family represented by their wives. The few women responsible for a family's land, called *ejidatarias*, are widows, and none attends the monthly meetings of the governing body. "Why not?" I asked one woman elder in San Marcos. "Are you crazy!?" she joked. "No woman would want to step in that building. I prefer to stay here in my house." If there is an important decision to be made by the *ejidatarios*, both *ejidatarios* living in the United States—the majority of all *ejidatarios*—and *ejidatarias* send their vote by proxy. While distance prevents *ejidatarios* in the

United States from attending meetings, *ejidatarias* stay away because they are uncomfortable in a space that is dominated by men.

Today in the rancho, because of migration, patrilocality is a challenge to sustain, and family has taken on new and shifting configurations that are again gendered, though in much different ways. Migration is resulting in a move toward smaller family units—nuclear families, female-headed households, and small groupings of cross-generational relations. With men primarily in the north, and women and children concentrated in Mexico, mothers often live with young children in the rancho while fathers live with elder sons in the United States, mothers-in-law and daughters-in-law may live under one roof without husbands, small groups of men make up all-male residences in *el norte*, and children stay with grandmothers and aunts for extended periods in Mexico.

When men migrate, married women are increasingly likely to stay in or return to their parents' home while their husbands are away for months or years, another shift from previous decades. Even in families with fewer migrants, such as the Luna family, daughters may stay with or return to their parents' homes (with or without their husbands). Jazmín, a young woman in her twenties, told me that she is very happy to be living with her parents in Mexico, rather than with her in-laws in a neighboring town. When her husband went to New Mexico just after their wedding, Jazmín decided to stay with her parents rather than following the tradition of moving to her husband's community. Jazmín said that her mother is a great help with her toddler son, and she feels fortunate that she does not have to live in the same house as her mother-in-law, whom she described as "*loca*" or "crazy."

Diana is another woman living in her natal family's compound. After Diana's husband requested a divorce and refused to support his three young children, Diana moved back to her parents' home. Diana's siblings were outraged that her husband had deserted her, especially because they were in Albuquerque with him at the time and because, as one brother described to me, they had made every effort to facilitate his migration. So, Diana's siblings began sending money, which Diana used toward the construction of a house on her family's property. The house is still in progress, but Diana said she looks forward to its completion. In the meantime, Diana and her children will continue to live with her parents. Diana said that there are many benefits to living with her parents, the children's grandparents—they can help her with childcare, and because most of her siblings are in the United States, it is reassuring for everyone in the family to have Diana living close to their parents. Although the majority of families in the rancho continue to live in patrilocal residences, among the younger generation, especially residents in their twenties, alternative kinship arrangements are becoming increasingly common.

In the United States, all-male households exemplify how residence patterns are transforming kinship relations. Most notably, wider ties among family and community members have taken on increased importance. While extended families have lived on compounds in San Marcos and neighboring communities throughout the last century, today "family" is extended further horizontally and can even include community members who are not relatives. As the experiences of Juan Carlos demonstrate, apartments of males are commonly made up of relatives and friends—great-uncles and grand-nephews, second cousins, neighbors, and acquaintances from nearby ranchos. In a transnational context, who constitutes "family" expands as migrants construct "home" over large distances.

Even as family is increasingly extended, nuclear family households are becoming quite common, especially when women and children migrate to the United States. While women may move into all-male apartments when they first arrive, men view this arrangement as temporary and aim to move out of group residences as soon as they are able to after their family's arrival. For example, when one of Juan Carlos' uncles brought his wife and four children to Albuquerque; they lived in one of the bedrooms of the males' apartment for a few months, just long enough to find an affordable apartment for the family. In the United States, most couples with children establish nuclear family households—parents and children living in an apartment or home apart from other family members. Such kinship arrangements are quite different than in ranchos, where networks of family members and neighbors are an important part of daily life.

Migrants try to re-create family compounds in the United States, usually by having families live in adjacent apartments or buying houses in the same housing development. For example, two families rented units in an Albuquerque duplex. When I visited them in their homes, I was struck by the similarities to living arrangements I had seen in the rancho. Cousins moved freely between the two homes, and the sisters often went to one another's kitchen to help prepare large meals. Because these two families were living adjacent to one another, extended family get-togethers often took place at the duplex. Family members would come from all over the city for celebrations and special events, or even just to drop by for a visit. However, such arrangements are relatively few in number among transmigrants living in the United States. Overall, transnational migration is resulting in kinship configurations that are quite different from the ways family was arranged on the rancho fifty years ago. Similarly, building community after migration requires creative strategies and is different from connecting with family and neighbors in Mexico.

When considering these shifts in family and community—as Mexicans go from relatively autonomous actors in an agricultural economy to migrant laborers within global capitalism and as extended, patrilocal families organized around farms become small, often nuclear family groupings—it is useful to revisit Marxist ideas about the role of families (see Engels 1942), especially Marxist-feminist theorizing about women's particular loss of power under capitalism (e.g., Sargent 1981). The "double day" continues, accompanied by new forms of the unrecognized economic contributions of women. And while recent work that considers the gendered character of global capital has focused on the feminization of migration (see e.g., Donato et al. 2006; Ehrenreich and Hochschild 2002; Hondagneu-Sotelo 2007; Parreñas 2001), the case of Mexico also shows its inverse: the feminization of staying or not moving (chap. 6) and a care chain—and a "care drain" (Hochschild 2002: 17)—that extends in two directions, to and from developing countries. Above all, gendered residences in the U.S.-Mexico transnation reassert anthropological insights about kinship and relatedness. Far from early anthropological frameworks that searched for the universals of family ties (see Collier, Rosaldo, and Yanagisako 1997), transnational kinship reveals the flexibility of residence and relatedness (Carsten 2000, 2004), as well as gendered power imbalances that persist.

Constructing Home

The ways that transnational Mexicans construct family, domestic spaces, and residences are indeed shifting as a result of migration.[1] So, too, are notions of home. As one migrant, Isaac, described days before the swearing-in ceremony when he formally became a U.S. citizen: "You could say that half of my home is here, and half is in Mexico. I have two homes . . . I am divided." Isaac's words, like those of Lucía at the beginning of this chapter, capture the complexities in situating family and locating home for transnational migrants. Individual narratives underscore the intersection of as well as the divergence between nation, place, and family in the lives of transnational Mexicans.

Transnational family ties create home that both transcends and is divided by the U.S.-Mexico border. Such fluidity and fragmentation generates myriad experiences, and the narratives of transnational Mexicans reveal ambivalent expressions of home: home is at once a geographic place and a symbolic space, one's domicile and where one identifies as a member of the community, the place where one currently lives and the multiple distinct locales where family members reside. The narratives of transmigrants express home along three axes, which are sometimes parallel, sometimes divergent, and often intersecting: home-as-nation, home-as-place, and home-as-family. As transnational Mexicans move between Mexico and the United States, delineating community, maintaining family ties, and ultimately, locating home become increasingly complex processes.

Defining "home" is never a simple task, and for anyone, home is characterized by multiple meanings, both tangible and ethereal. Home can be a physical space, the place where you are from, where you are comfortable, where you feel you belong. In a world marked by economic and political globalization and unprecedented human migrations, theoretical work has encouraged us to rethink home in a transnational context. The anthropologist Karen Fog Olwig describes how "sustaining a home in a deterritorialized world" has considerable implications for ethnographic research and calls for a reconceptualization of home that, paradoxically, situates movement (Olwig 1997: 17). Similarly, the social theorists Nigel Rapport and Andrew Dawson suggest that home is "where one best knows oneself—where 'best' means 'most', even if not always 'happiest'" (Rapport and Dawson 1998: 9). As the personal narratives of Mexican (im)migrants illustrate, home is imbued with ambiguity, and discourses of belonging express contradictions and congruity, fluidity and fragmentation.

Home as Nation

Transnational Mexicans must negotiate the contradictions and complexities inherent in living within and constructing a physical and imaginative home in two distinct nation-states. An either/or model for national belonging does not adequately serve transnational migrants: multiple loyalties are possible and, arguably, inevitable. An individual may identify as a Mexican and an American simultaneously, experience a sense of belonging to both countries, or express loyalties to two (or potentially more) countries in different ways and/or at particular moments. As discussed, transnational Mexicans repeatedly describe themselves as "half here, half there," as well as "from both sides." Such tropes of national belonging underscore the complicated formations of the nation as home within a transnational space.

By situating home in both/either Mexico and/or the United States, transmigrants express malleable notions of national membership that both challenge and are confined by limits established by individual states. Luis, a U.S. citizen, described how his national "home" is situated according to context:

> If someone asks, "What is your nationality?," I would say, "I am Mexican." But if someone else asks me, I might say, "I am an American citizen." It depends who asks me. If an American asks me, a police officer, for example, "I am an American." If immigration stops me and asks, I would say my nationality is from here [the United States].

He further explained that in general when talking or interacting with Mexicans, he identifies as a Mexican, and in exchanges with Americans, he calls himself "American." Mexicans understand plural "citizenships" to be an asset, an advantage when maneuvering within more than one nation-state. As one mother explained, "It is good to have both." She said that her children are fortunate to have two nations as home. She explained that they will have more choices and multiple options because of dual nationality—they will speak two languages, have many work opportunities, and, ultimately, be able to call both nations "home."

Home as Place

Home is often associated with a geographic place: the roof over your head, the place you grew up, the nation in which you were born. Anthropologists have historically relied on a bounded and narrow definition of place (see Hastrup and Olwig 1997). In the analysis of place in a transnational context, ethnographers may have overcorrected, focusing on the deterriorialization associated with transience and mobility, at the expense of a nuanced reconceptualization of space within global flows. Indeed, specific places hold importance for communities (Basso 1996), and there is a need to study place in transnational lives: "Instead of stopping with the notion of deterritorialization . . . we need to theorize how space is being *re*territorialized in the contemporary world" (Gupta and Ferguson 1997a: 50). Even as the practices of transnational subjects challenge the notion of inherent or natural ties to a geographic place, physical spaces take on renewed significance.

Because of the intersection of imagined and actual movement between multiple locales of home, distinguishing between metaphorical and geographical places can be difficult. An example are the many discourses in which individuals identify their "*raíces*" or roots in Mexico. Such roots are often metaphorically described as ancestral ties to Mexico linked through "*sangre*" or blood, but one's roots are also geographically situated in a particular physical place. As the anthropologist Liisa Malkki has argued, "people are often thought of, and think of themselves, as being rooted in place and as deriving their identity from that rootedness" (Malkki 1992: 27). Consider the words of Cito—notably, Cito repeated the following phrase throughout our interview: "My desire has always been—alive or dead—to return to Mexico." He continued, "I am a Mexican and an American citizen, but I belong in my country. I will never deny that. Mexico is everything. I think for all Mexicans, home is Mexico, like for you Americans, home is the United States." He discussed his desire to repatriate his body to Mexico after his death in order to be buried in his hometown. He explained to me that despite the fact that the process would be costly and logistically complicated, he felt it would be important for him to return to his homeland and to be physically placed in the ground of his home community.

Cito's explanation of the many ways he "goes home" further explicates the interplay between physical and imaginative place:

When I am here, I think of going home as returning to my house [in the United States]. When I take a trip to Mexico, and I am in my house there, that is where I go home to. Sometimes, when I think about going home, I think about going to my house in Mexico, to see my parents, even though the reality is my house is here.

Whether it is returning to one's house at the end of the day, visiting family and friends in one's hometown, or arranging for one's body to be buried in a particular place, homecomings are rooted in spaces with both literal and symbolic significance, and are increasingly difficult to attain. "Home," for transnational Mexicans—as for all of us—manifests in multiple and constantly shifting configurations. Indeed, in this world of unprecedented transnational movement, people "are always and yet never 'at home'" (Rapport and Dawson 1998: 6).

Home as Family

Above all, as migrants experience lives that are increasingly transnational, family often trumps nation and place in the construction of home. María stated, "For me, home is my family together, living together . . . with everyone, your spouse and your children. If someone lives alone, it is not a home, maybe a house but not a home. For us, home is family." Family relations are perceived as one of the central constitutive dimensions of home. As family extends across borders, home is characterized by new forms. Transmigrants construct home as mobile, building home through translocal rituals and family events, transnational communication and travel, and perceptions of connectedness despite distance and over time.

Isaac, mentioned earlier, is a naturalized U.S. citizen who first migrated from Mexico nearly twenty years ago. Two of his children, teenagers and native U.S. citizens, currently live with their grandparents in Mexico, while two younger children live with Isaac and his wife in the United States. Isaac explained how his home spans immense geographic distance, even as it is split by the U.S.-Mexico border: "For me personally, my home is Mexico. But now, I have two families . . . my parents are there, [my children], my brothers and sisters, but my wife and [two of] my children are here. I have—how can I describe it?—I have two halves." Similarly, Jorge told me that "both places are home . . . you have family there and here" while Lucía described how her family is "half there and half here." When families are divided by an international boundary, the process of situating home becomes increasingly complex.

The narratives and lives of transnational Mexicans illustrate the challenges to creating home and structuring family within a world of movement. Transmigrants express home as nation and home as place, but especially home as family, underscoring how "home" is imbued with contradictions, ambiguity, and ambivalence, and, above all, how kinship is intertwined with transnational life. Family structures are characterized by both consistency and transformation as migrant families and communities extend across the U.S.-Mexico border. Among transnational Mexicans, expressions of home and configurations of family are made up of parts and totalities, inconsistencies and continuities, divisions and connections. Home and family can be, as Lucía described, "*mitad allá, mitad aquí*/half there, half here," as well as, in the words of Victor, "*de ambos lados*/from both sides."

Family "Reunification"

In a room filled with colorful balloons and the remains of a *piñata*, the mood was, for the most part, celebratory. The guest of honor, a three-year-old girl in a cloud of white taffeta, was opening her gifts, relishing an enormous heart-shaped lollipop. Although a crowd of family and friends was gathered around the birthday girl, another smaller grouping was in the kitchen, speaking in hushed voices and comforting Dulce, whose husband, Francisco, had been deported the previous week after a raid at his workplace. "We will find a solution," Dulce's brother told me with conviction. "But this is a difficult time for our family." Most of the Laredo family is undocumented—Francisco, Dulce, and their two eldest children, Javier and Mina—although their youngest daughter, Beatriz, is a U.S. citizen. The Laredo family reunited in the United States after Francisco had been living alone in Albuquerque for several years. Dulce said that the time apart was unbearable and though she thought it was the best decision at the time, now she wondered if their move was worth the risks.

In the months after the deportation, Francisco's and Dulce's siblings put together funds to cover the cost of a *coyote* with papers, choosing to spend the extra money to have Francisco cross with documents because it is considered more secure. Eventually Francisco was able to return to the United States. Today, Dulce, Francisco, and their children again—though tenuously—live as a family "reunited" in the United States, but they still fear deportation and agonize over what would happen to the children should they be taken into state custody. Javier, who left Mexico when he was young, told me he would like to visit Mexico, but he looks forward to attending the high school down the street from his Albuquerque apartment. He said he would not want to return to the rancho permanently, joking that he has no idea how to farm pinto beans. Mina, who was an infant when she arrived in the United States, has no recollection of her country of origin.

The experiences of the Laredo family demonstrate that the state's reach into family life is strong and point to some of the contradictory dimensions of U.S. immigration policies.[1] Actions of the U.S. state can impact, construct, define, (re)produce, reunite, and/or divide families. More often than not, it is through state-migrant interactions that family is (re)constituted in a transnational space, and exclusion itself stems from the state's prerogative to "regulate membership according to family ties" (Stevens 1999: 7). An emphasis on the multiple experiences of transnational migrants within family networks and as actors vis-à-vis the state reveals both state actions and the (re)structuring of transnational families. The ethnographic study of the negotiations between Mexican migrants and the state, and especially the production of (il)legality, provides a starting point for understanding how the U.S. state structures migrant families, as well as the ways transnational Mexicans navigate the shifting terrain of state power, building lives and kin relations in the U.S.-Mexico transnation.

Chapter 2 considered how family relations guide and change through migrations; this chapter focuses on the notion of "family reunification"—an underlying principle of U.S. immigration policy—to understand state actions and how the state penetrates family life. State control can, for example, influence decisions to migrate or not, family residence patterns, and migrations that separate or reunite family members. Family reunification can include state-sanctioned and state-regulated family reunification, as well as the multiple ways that migrants construct and reunite family outside of state controls. While Mexicans and the U.S. state privilege family reunification, it is in clearly distinct ways, and ideas of when and how it should happen often diverge. Paradoxically, U.S. immigration policy based on family reunification can both join and divide family members. A focus on how migrants navigate state regimes and state categories of "legal" and "illegal" uncovers this contradictory character of U.S. family "reunification."

Here, the focus shifts from emic understandings and experiences of family life to examine state practices as they play out on the ground. There are multiple layers of power—including individual action, family strategies, and state policies and practices—that coincide, cooperate, and conflict with one another as families come together and are divided within a transnational space. The ethnographic study of the everyday lives of transnational families can turn attention from individual migrants to the conditions and constraints within which they maneuver, to "investigate critically what the law actually accomplishes" (De Genova 2002: 432). Problematizing the notion that migrants act independently or disconnected from structures uncovers how the actions of migrants are shaped by state power, a theme that runs throughout this book. Despite laws that focus on migrants as individuals, transnational Mexicans are always embedded in families and communities, and, importantly, state regimes.

The State of the State

The concept of "the state" has been the focus of a substantial body of anthropological research (e.g., Alonso 1994; Kearney 1991, 1995; Joseph and Nugent 1994; Nagengast 1994, among others). My research augments ethnographic study of the ways that state regimes, institutions, and agents interpret, implement, and/or extend immigration laws (Coutin 2000, 2003, 2007; Heyman 1995, 1999a, 1999b, 2000, 2002; Maril 2004). The perspective of transnational Mexicans, a view from those directly impacted by U.S. policies and practices, contributes to understandings of the complexity of state structures and multiple state actors. While "the state is an object whose reality will be denied if we focus exclusively on deconstructed representations of it" (Wilson and Donnan 1998: 8), it is nonetheless important that the construct be scrutinized through experiences of migrants. Indeed, "there is an autonomous and extraordinarily powerful entity called the state" (Nagengast 1994), and anthropologists have much to gain by considering the state through ethnographic study.

Social theorists have turned to the many facets and manifestations of the state. Les Field defines the state as the "institutionalized, organizational apparatus that governs a group of individuals defined as citizens within a variously conceptualized spatial territory" (Field 1999: 2), while Nira Yuval-Davis and Floya Anthias call it "a body of institutions which are centrally organized around the intentionality of control with a given apparatus of enforcement (juridical and repressive) at its command and basis" (Yuval-Davis and Anthias 1989: 5). The state also operates as "the guardian of national borders, the arbiter of citizenship, and the entity responsible for foreign policy" (Kearney 1995: 548). Michael Kearney identifies that "the fundamental project of the state . . . is to elaborate and resolve the contradiction of differentiation and unity" (Kearney 1991: 55), an agenda that especially plays out in the lives of (im)migrants.

In addition, the state is a constellation of multiple individual and institutional actors, "a multilayered, contradictory, translocal ensemble of institutions, practices, and people" (Sharma and Gupta 2006: 6). Kitty Calavita encourages scholars to unpack "the state" by examining "specific state agencies, institutions, and cadres of state managers" (Calavita 1992: 175). The state also "incorporates cultural and political forms, representations, discourse, practices and activities, and specific technologies and organizations of power" (Nagengast 1994: 116). The state, then, is a complex—intricate and yet at times awkward—apparatus of power with multiple and conflicting cultural, political, economic, and ideological ends.

Previous studies of transnationalism have been criticized for an overemphasis on the weakening of the state (see Aretxaga 2003), although globalization "is not only compatible with statehood; it has actually fueled the desire for it" (Aretxaga 2003: 395; see also Hess 2009). In response to such critique, recent scholarship within anthropology theorizes transnational encounters as "friction" (Tsing 2005), laden with "growing inequality" and "exclusion" (Appadurai 2006: x). Reconsiderations of state power capture its erosion as well as reformulations of state control (e.g., Kearney 1998, Rosas 2007). My analysis draws on this shift in research about the state, situating family life within the context of transmigration that is increasingly defined through state power.

For Mexican (im)migrant families, the U.S. nation-state is ever present: at the highly militarized U.S.-Mexico border, through immigration policies and practices, and increasingly through workplace raids, border apprehensions, detention, and deportation. The state also penetrates family life through the many bureaucratic processes required to apply for visas, file for residency, and naturalize. In many ways, the state perpetuates itself through its diverse manifestations and an assortment of agents who carry out its multiple, often conflicting and/or unformulated goals. State power is explicitly present in the lives of undocumented migrants, although the state's reach also extends to documented migrants, including those who have naturalized or were born as U.S. citizens. Indeed, through the post-9/11 erosion of rights, U.S. permanent residents and even U.S. citizens are also susceptible to the workings of the state. The U.S. state's presence in the daily lives of all transnational Mexicans is potent, and at certain times and under particular circumstances, severe or even inescapable.

While my work is informed by this scholarship that directly studies state agencies and actors, my analysis of the state comes at related questions from a different perspective: the seemingly intimate gendered and family lives of transnational Mexicans. Here, my focus is on the ways the state's presence plays out in family life. The words and experiences of migrants provide a particular and telling glimpse of state policies and the work of state agents. Given that such state processes often gain strength through their obscurity, the study of the everyday lives of transnational families can make visible the character of particular state actions. Such ethnography is fruitful to look "inside the state" (Calavita 1992) and to explicate state processes that may otherwise be difficult for researchers to "reach" (Rhodes 2006). The perspective of transnational Mexicans, a view from those directly impacted by U.S. policies and practices, contributes to an understanding of the complexity of state structures and multiple state actors.

Family Reunification?

Analysis of the character of "family reunification" as it is constructed and formulated through state action provides a way to examine contradictions within U.S. state policies and practices. The Immigration and Nationality Act of 1965 eliminated national-origin quotas and established a new principle for U.S. immigration—family unification (DeSipio and de la Garza 1998: 42). Such state-administered family reunification can bring (certain) families together, and yet, state laws and practices systematically divide families. A focus on this underlying principle of U.S. immigration law outlines the ways that unofficial or de facto family reunification is challenged or undermined explicitly because of state practices. State policies have changed and restructured family transnationally, impacting lengths of stay, creating geographic divisions, and encouraging families to reunite outside of formal or "legal" means.

The 1965 legislation—coupled with amnesty provided by the Immigration Reform and Control Act (IRCA) of 1986—has had a profound impact on the migration trajectories of transnational Mexicans. These policies have, to varying degrees, facilitated migration and touched the lives of nearly every transnational Mexican family. The contradictions within state policies and practices are multiple and nuanced. Current U.S. immigration law does, in fact, privilege "family"—albeit a state-defined construction of kinship—and the (re)unification of family members. At the same time, however, directly because of state policies and practices, migration to and from the United States actually divides families and undermines family structures. By dividing family members into categories of "legal" and "illegal," the U.S. state is ever-present in family life. Post-IRCA migration has been characterized, paradoxically, by conditions in which an increasing number of people can "legalize," specifically through family ties, as the undocumented population and the number of mixed-status families grow, a pattern that has intensified since 9/11 and that continues to characterize migration from Mexico.

Families United

Underlying my argument is the assumption that U.S. state policies divide families, although they can unite transnational Mexicans as well. Consider the story of Marisa. Her common-law husband, Vicente, traveled to the United States with plans to send money back to Marisa and their three young children. The money never came, however, and after several months Vicente announced that he was in love with another woman, and that he had no plans to support his children financially. Faced with this crisis, Marisa put her children under the care of her mother, the children's grandmother, and left with her older brother for Albuquerque. She began working and sending remittances home. As Marisa recounted her first year in Albuquerque, she fought back tears: "It was a very difficult time . . . I was so far from my children. I will never allow us to be separated like that again."

But Marisa's experience took a positive turn—one that impacted her family significantly—that was directly shaped by U.S. immigration laws. After ten months in New Mexico, she met Pedro, a Mexican national who naturalized as a U.S. citizen. The couple began dating and soon moved in together. After six months, Marisa and Pedro decided to marry and to bring Marisa's children to live with them in Albuquerque. Through Marisa's marriage to Pedro, Marisa and her children were able to become U.S. permanent residents. "Now, looking back, I am grateful that I came here. Now that I have a life with Pedro, I realize that my difficulties were worth it." The union between Marisa and Pedro altered the legal status of Marisa and her children: the marriage provided a path to documented immigration and allowed her to build a life for herself and her children in the United States. As Marisa's mother explained to me, Pedro "opened the door for the family . . . by marrying Marisa and adopting the children, he took them out of the shadows."

Clearly, families can reunite through the U.S. state's official process. Migrants bring family members to the United States through these "legal" channels, utilizing U.S. policies and the state-authorized process when possible. In this sense, the U.S. state plays a role in unifying family members, as well as facilitating additional immigration. In their ethnographic study of Haitian migration, Nina Glick Schiller and Georges Eugene Fouron have shown that "rediscovering and revitalizing family connections is a transnational strategy" (Glick Schiller and Fouron 2001: 61). And indeed, among transnational Mexicans documented (im)migration to the United States, with few exceptions, depends on family relations: marriage to a U.S. citizen or resident and/or petitioning for family members through the Immigration and Nationality Act of 1965 is essentially the only way for working-poor Mexicans to migrate with documents. This is certainly the case among migrants I have interviewed; every individual I know who has transitioned from undocumented to documented status since amnesty after IRCA has done so through family ties or marriage.

Within a framework that links immigration policies to the family, family relations and particularly marriage can be potent migration strategies that demonstrate migrants' flexibility vis-à-vis the U.S. state. U.S. policies can work in the favor of (im)migrants: through marriage and by petitioning for relatives, transnational Mexicans may secure their individual position within the United States, and perhaps more importantly, strengthen family ties that reach across the U.S.-Mexico border. As the experiences of Marisa illustrate, marrying a U.S. citizen and petitioning for a family member are linked: marriage creates new family ties and establishes relationships through which additional family members may also obtain U.S. permanent residency. When Marisa married Pedro, for example, she and her children became U.S. permanent residents. They intend to naturalize as U.S. citizens and will then be in a position to petition for other kin, such as Marisa's adult siblings, sometime in the future.

U.S. policies encourage immigration through family relations, and establish marriage as a path to legal U.S. national membership. Marriage, and then the forging of wider kin networks, establishes a chain of immigration. The experiences of Rocío further illustrate this point. Twenty years ago, Rocío's family was struggling to make a living through agriculture. Rocío's husband—once a bracero in the United States—had died in an accident, leaving her a single mother with five children to support. Rocío's eldest son, Mateo, often talked with his mother about going to the United States, and as worried as she was to have him leave, Rocío knew that he had few options. Eventually Mateo did make the trip north, crossed without documents, and lived and worked in the United States for several years.

In New Mexico, Mateo met and later married a U.S. citizen. After several years, he naturalized as a U.S. citizen himself and then began petitioning for family members, including Rocío. Rocío recently told me that she hoped to improve her English, primarily so that she can understand her daughters-in-law, several of whom are U.S. citizens who do not speak Spanish well. As she explained, it is in her best interest to learn English, because she is concerned that her daughters-in-law might be insulting her without her knowledge. After all, she told me, it is preferable to hear such criticism firsthand. Rocío's desire to learn English illustrates the significant changes that have taken place in her family over the past two decades. Today, four of Rocío's children are married to U.S. permanent residents or U.S. citizens, and the majority of her grandchildren were born in the United States. As Rocío's family demonstrates, family reunification facilitates transnational movement, and marriage frequently leads to further (im)migration.

Although "family reunification" principles guide U.S. immigration policy, migrants such as Pedro and Marisa, as well as Rocío and her adult children and their spouses, face state regulation in their everyday lives. Throughout the process of securing residency, particular family members may spend years apart and their movement may be repeatedly restricted by the U.S. state; even when individual family members acquire U.S. permanent residency or citizenship, the state limits the movement of transmigrants. The state's hold on family life is strong, pushing families to work within state bureaucracies when possible but also to operate outside of state control. While (im)migrants reunite their families through state processes when they are able, such options are not available to all transnational Mexicans, and so migrants frequently reunite families outside of the state's official procedures. State-sanctioned family reunification depends on state-enforced definitions of "resident" and "citizen," and within the current policy context, the majority of transnational Mexicans do not have access to family reunification through the U.S. state.

Families Interrupted

The state clearly disrupts family unification, in part because of the state's presence in family life. Although ostensibly designed to unite families, a lasting effect of the immigration legislation of 1965 is that the state—through increasing involvement and control—fractures family life among (im)migrant communities. The "reunification" of family members is required precisely because of the state's role in dividing families. Indeed, "we cannot analytically delink the operations of family regimes from the regulations of state and of capital" (Ong 1999: 113).

One primary way the state divides families is through its definitions of "family" itself, constructs that delineate and regulate kinship relations. The U.S. state and Mexican migrants interpret and understand family in multiple and often contradictory ways, and there is an ongoing tension that centers on state attempts to define, and confine, family. Transnational Mexican families perceive of kin and prioritize family in ways that are quite different from the way "family" is defined through U.S. policies. This is evident in the specific priorities the U.S. state provides to immigrants petitioning for family members. Since the 1965 legislation, spouses, minor children, and parents of U.S. citizens have been given priority, while the siblings and adult children of U.S. citizens, and spouses, minor children, and parents of permanent residents, have been permitted to immigrate on a more limited basis (DeSipio and de la Garza 1998: 139). Such criteria are often different from, and generally not as inclusive as, the ways that migrants actually conceive of family.

For example, one migrant, Iván, was able to bring his wife and four of his children to the United States through legal channels, while his unmarried twenty-one-year-old daughter was ineligible for residency and had to remain in Mexico with her grandmother. Iván said that this was a cause of serious stress for his family, particularly because it is common for children in rural Mexico to live with their parents until they marry. The construct of a twenty-one-year-old as an adult who should live independent of her parents is problematic within Mexican families and does not accurately reflect how Mexican (im)migrants think about family. These understandings of kin are distinctively gendered (see chaps. 4 and 5). Similarly, within transnational families, adult siblings and adult children are often considered "immediate" family members, although they are not defined as such by the U.S. government.

A reunified family from the perspective of a Mexican national, then, does not necessarily correspond with, and may diverge significantly from, definitions of family as constructed by the U.S. state. One of the effects of state-defined family reunification is that extended and "nuclear" transnational families, as is the case with the Laredo family, are made up of individuals with different immigration statuses vis-à-vis the U.S. state. Mixed-status families reveal the contradictory character of U.S. policies, laws that are ostensibly aimed at reunifying families.

The State of Relatedness: (Il)legality and Mixed-Status Families

Members of the extended Laredo family, described earlier, embody several distinct immigration status positions as defined by the U.S. state: Dulce, Francisco, and their two teenage children are undocumented migrants; their youngest daughter, Beatriz, is a U.S. citizen, born in the United States. Both Dulce and Francisco have siblings who are undocumented, U.S. permanent residents, and naturalized U.S. citizens. Their nieces and nephews, like their own children, have different immigration statuses: some are U.S. citizens, several are undocumented, and some are in the process of obtaining permanent residency. While U.S. immigration policy focuses on individual migrants, individuals are always embedded within and connected to families and communities. A focus on migrants as individual actors, with little discussion of the context within which they move and act, perpetuates what De Genova identifies as the simultaneous "visibility of 'illegal immigrants'" and "invisibility of the law" (De Genova 2002: 431). A focus solely on the actions of individual migrants obscures central players in the structuring of transnational families: the U.S. state and its agents, and particularly how state policies and practices play out in the lives of migrant families.

The backdrop to families divided transnationally is the state's authority to categorize individual migrants and the construction of immigration status. It is through definitions of who constitutes a legitimate migrant in the first place—the "discursive formation of 'illegality'" (De Genova 2002: 432)—that state power is particularly strong in disrupting family life. Much of the state's power to penetrate kin relations of Mexican migrants derives from definitions of migrants' status within the United States. Through the production of illegality, categories of "citizen," "resident," "illegal alien," and "criminal alien" shape family and create the potential and probability, as well as the unlikelihood or impossibility, of "legal" family reunification.

Essentially every transnational family is a mixed-status family, made up of individuals with different immigration statuses within the United States: this is a reality for siblings, parents, and children as well as extended family members. Families may include members who are birthright or naturalized U.S. citizens, U.S. permanent residents, unauthorized migrants, individuals in the process of applying for an immigration status change, or people in the country under nonpermanent visas, such as tourist or temporary worker visas. The Pew Hispanic Center estimates that as of 2008, there were 8.8 million people living in the United States within mixed status families, of which 4 million were U.S. citizen children (Passel and Cohn 2009). Mixed status families are configured in diverse ways, and immigration statuses can vary in a partnership, within a nuclear or extended family, or across generations. For example, among couples, one partner might be undocumented while the other partner is a U.S. citizen or resident. It is common for siblings to have different immigration statuses, for parents to be undocumented while their children are U.S. citizens, or for U.S. permanent residents or citizens to have children, typically adult children, who are living in the United States without authorization. Grandparents and grandchildren, aunts, uncles, nieces, nephews, and cousins are likely to have a mixture of statuses as well.

Despite the fact that family reunification is a foundational element of current U.S. immigration policy, in practice such regulations further separate transnational families by focusing on each member of a family rather than on family units: immigrants must file for residency or citizenship as individuals. The state, then, derives its power to define and divide families by interacting with individuals rather than families. A fundamental trait of immigration policy is "that it singles out the border and the individual as the sites for regulatory enforcement" (Sassen 1996a: 10). It is precisely this focus on the individual that creates mixed-status families. Virtually all members of trans-national families—albeit to varying degrees—are within the state's reach, including people who migrate and people who do not, undocumented and documented migrants, permanent residents, naturalized U.S. citizens, and individuals born in the United States, explicating that government is indeed concerned with its subjects "in their relations, their links" (Foucault 1977: 93). The U.S. state focuses on individual family members, extracting them from the context of family and community. This further isolates individuals from their family, especially from the perspective of the state, and continues to divide families.

In constructing individual subjects as "legal" or "illegal," the state regulates who may cross national borders with authorization and who is formally excluded. The U.S.-Mexico border, therefore, serves as a physical barrier to family reunification. Increased militarization of the border has ushered in shifts in migration practices—changes that have directly impacted how, when, where, and how often people cross the border, going both north and south—as well as "new forms of insecurity" (Center for Comparative Immigration Studies 2005) for migrants whose lives straddle the U.S.-Mexico divide. Although crossing the border has long been risky for undocumented migrants, transnational Mexicans perceive undocumented migration as even more dangerous in the post-9/11 context. Migrants express deep anxiety about how best to cross or have their children cross as they contemplate ways to build transnational families despite shifting and increasingly stringent border enforcement.

The state's construction of immigration status results in the state's threat of, and ability to carry out, deportation as well as deportation itself. As the experiences of the Laredo family demonstrate, actualized deportations physically separate families. Migrants are indeed aware of how the state constructs deportability and the ways it threatens family life among families with members who are undocumented or of mixed statuses. Understandably, many parents express concerns about their own tenuous legal status and/or the status of their children. Parents speculate about separations from their children should they themselves be deported, and they fear the especially frightening scenario of having their children apprehended or placed in state custody. Deportability can lead parents to make the decision to situate family in two nation-states, often separating parents and children.

Besides the more direct state actions that keep families apart—such as ascribing legal status, creating an elaborate system of family reunification, prioritizing categories of family relations, and deporting individual family members—there are other disciplining tactics arguably aimed at families on the part of the state, what De Genova calls "excessive and extraordinary forms of policing" (De Genova 2002: 439). In addition to raids at workplaces, U.S. Immigration and Customs Enforcement (ICE) agents also police outside churches and schools with large migrant populations (Ramirez 2005)—a clear assault on family life. For families with undocumented members who are living together in the United States, there are many fears about working, moving, and simply leading day-to-day lives without documents (see Coutin 2000). Family life is indeed "shadowed" (Chavez 1992), causing parents to avoid interacting with government entities if at all possible, even when they are victims of crime or their children have urgent medical needs.

For example, in one family, a couple's adolescent son ingested a large dose of over-the-counter cold medicine. The boy's friends at the local junior high school said it would be "fun," but when he became very ill, he told his parents what had happened. The parents were frightened to visit the emergency room because of rumors that ICE was working with hospital officials to find unauthorized migrants. Instead of taking such a risk, the boy's mother called the family doctor in Mexico, read the ingredients of the medication from the packaging to him, and followed the doctor's instructions in treating her son. In families of mixed statuses vis-à-vis the U.S. state, "spaces of nonexistence" (Coutin 2000: 27) define daily life. Given the current legal climate, it is surprising the extent to which transnational families are united *despite* the U.S.-Mexico border.

The lengthy bureaucratic process of family reunification can also have a disciplinary effect. Rocío's experience applying for residency illustrates how the state penetrates family life in multiple ways. While the process can "reunite" certain family members, reunifying family through state channels also causes stress for family members who worry about whether U.S. permanent residency or citizenship will indeed be granted, restricts movement while individuals file (a process that can take years), and creates anxiety and exerts control at appointments with state officials by placing the burden on families to "prove" the validity of family and marital relations and questioning individuals in arbitrary ways. There are also cases in which people are being deported while completing the steps necessary to naturalize as U.S. citizens (Preston 2008) or in the process of applying for a change in their immigration status.

I witnessed an event that demonstrates how the state disciplines migrants even after they have (ostensibly) successfully maneuvered through the state's bureaucracy when I attended a swearing-in ceremony of one of my ESL students, Jesús. Prior to the ceremony, Jesús had told me that he was extremely nervous about the event and about securing citizenship so that he could petition for his wife and children; indeed, the immigration status of several family members depended on Jesús securing citizenship. After everything he had been through processing paperwork with the then INS, it seemed unimaginable to him that he would actually become a U.S. citizen. He asked me if government officials could deny him citizenship at the ceremony, and he expressed his concern with the rigid language of the oath. He inquired about what would happen if, for example, Mexico and the United States went to war—would he be expected to fight for the United States against his home country? While I tried to reassure him that such a conflict was unlikely, his question underscores the dilemmas transnational Mexicans who naturalize as U.S. citizens face.

When Jesús signed in on the morning of the ceremony, the agent asked him if he had traveled outside the country in the past six months. "Yes," replied Jesús. "I was in Mexico for two weeks visiting family." The state official looked him in the eye and asked with a serious expression: "You didn't kill anyone while you were there, did you?" After a pause, the agent burst out laughing as Jesús looked at me with horror. Such disciplinary measures continued throughout the day. Even as the ceremony honorees held up their right hands and repeated the oath, officials walked up and down the auditorium aisles, policing these new citizens. Jesús' fears about the power of the government and the potential of the state to deny him citizenship were in many ways well-founded. Given that the status of Jesús' wife and children hinged on his success naturalizing, he felt especially vulnerable throughout the process. It is through controls such as these that the state restrains not just individuals but also family members.

State power is never absolute, however, and this, too, is evident through an analysis of family reunification. Transnational families are the reality for millions of Mexican (im)migrants. Even as migrants are constrained by the state, and even as state power shapes family relations, transnational Mexicans destabilize the state's ability to absolutely control migration and define family. Families unite through "official" channels, and migrants also establish family reunification by circumventing a process that is directed by the U.S. state. Family reunification is, in fact, one of the central motivations for having women and children migrate. As the experiences of families illustrate, in many circumstances, transmigrants are forced to adhere to state-imposed definitions of immigrants and families, and yet migrants also structure family outside of state controls. Building on the concept of "autonomous migration" (Rodríguez 1996), transnational Mexicans' actions—always constrained by state power—can be read as a form of "autonomous family reunification." In this sense, as migrants build families across borders, they are "ahead of U.S. immigration policies in addressing the transnational realities of this region . . . through binational family/household and community networks" (Jonas 1996: 80). Still, following the anthropologist Susan Bibler Coutin, it is difficult to celebrate migrant agency in this context (Coutin 2000: 46).

Against the backdrop of state actions, a more nuanced understanding of the migrations of individual, always interconnected, family members comes into view. The unbalanced relationship between the U.S. state and people on the move is especially evident against the backdrop of "family reunification" and through a discussion of its contradictions. State maneuvers along the border and aimed at the individual directly impact migrants as members of families. Such an emphasis can extend analysis beyond the frame of the state versus the individual. State power certainly creates insecurity for individual migrants, but state actions also have profound implications for transnational families. Mexican (im)migrants are embedded within complex and significant networks of family ties, and it is difficult and misdirected to extract Mexican migrants from their experiences as members of families.

While the literature on "illegality" has significantly advanced an understanding of how states define and categorize members of the nation, much of the research has focused on migrants as a more or less uniform category. This study contributes to this body of work by specifically considering how the construction of illegality mediates kinship and family (dis)connections. The state's power to label has profound implications for asserting its control of transnational Mexicans, those who are documented as well as undocumented. The state exercises authority by defining "family" and by regulating kinship relations in numerous ways, although even policies without explicit ties to family can have deep and far-reaching effects on kin and home among transnational Mexicans. The state's categorization of immigrants has implications far beyond the individual, rippling throughout kin networks and playing a central role in constituting family itself.

Undocumented (im)migrants "have been denied fundamental human rights and many rudimentary social entitlements, consigned to an uncertain sociopolitical predicament, often with little or no recourse to any semblance of protection from the law" (De Genova 2002: 439). As family networks extend transnationally, there is a blurring of the documented and undocumented, in that Mexican families are typically made up of individual members with different statuses vis-à-vis the U.S. state. This analysis raises important questions about the rights of migrants as they construct family within a transnational space. The rights of families—or perhaps more aptly, the rights of migrants to organize and maintain partnerships and families how and where they wish within a transnational context—are at stake. The study of "family reunification" brings to the fore the power of the U.S. state to determine how people within—and indeed beyond—its borders construct family, highlighting the persistence of state presence in transnational family life.

PART II

Gendered Migrations

4

¡Ya Soy Hombre y Mujer!/
Now I Am a Man and a Woman!

On a hot, dusty spring afternoon in San Marcos, Rosa sat on her concrete living room floor, with her daughter and two of her sons, sorting through beans in preparation for planting. Their hands moved quickly, building a mound of lime green and separating out some shriveled beans and tossing them aside. Two burlap sacks of beans were propped up against a loveseat; one bag of beans was already sorted and one was filled with beans yet to be "cleaned." As she worked, Rosa recounted how her life had changed since her husband had gone to the United States three years earlier. "I take care of the fields, our animals . . . I'm currently painting our house. I have to do all the work my husband used to do. And, I'm still responsible for everything I did before— cooking, cleaning, caring for the children." Rosa sighed and looked up at me from the growing pile of beans. "It's a lot of work, isn't it?" I nodded, and we sat in silence as she reflected on her life. Then she smiled, threw back her head and laughed out loud, "Now I am a man *and* a woman!"

Rosa's declaration reflects the gendered moves—that is, the transformation of gender subjectivities—that accompany gendered migrations: the many negotiations, controls, conflicts, alliances, strategies, and maneuvers that coincide to construct gender subjectivities in a transnational space.[1] Rosa's observations about her changing way of life and the transforming role within her marriage reveal much about how gender identities are tied to the process of transnational movement. Constructions of manhood and womanhood, including expressions of multiple masculinities and femininities, are shifting as males and females migrate within a transnational space.

This part of the book focuses on "gender across borders" (Castellanos and Boehm 2008: 6) and the specifically gendered character of transnational migrations; it employs a feminist frame to study the lives of women and girls but also men and boys (e.g., Gutmann 1996, 2003; Pribilsky 2007). My analysis recognizes the shifting and fluid nature of gender performances and constructions (e.g., Abu-Lughod 1999; Alonso 1995; Butler 1989; Gutmann 1996; Kondo 1990; Ortner 1996; Stephen 1991, among others). As Ana María Alonso (1995, 76) describes:

> Gender is not only the social construction of sexual difference, that is, of distinctions between male and female, but also a primary site for the production and inscription of more general effects of power and meaning, a source of tropes that are key to the configuring of domination and subjection.

Gender is made (Ortner 1996), crafted (Kondo 1990), performed. Indeed, "gender is fluid over time [and] . . . within different social situations" (Stephen 1991: 253) and masculinity and femininity "are not original, natural, or embalmed states of being; they are gender categories whose precise meanings constantly shift, transform into each other, and ultimately make themselves into whole new entities" (Gutmann 1996: 21). Here, the focus is flexibility and mutability, particularly the many ways in which shifting gender subjectivities are linked to migration.

The study of gender constructions in a transnational context interrogates previous research about the benefits of migration for females. Scholars have suggested that migration—because it can destabilize rigid gender roles—is generally positive for women. This research builds on and also complicates this view. Migration results in a complex interplay between men and women—a series of negotiations through which women are exercising increased power in some circumstances but also facing the reassertion of male dominance. Similarly, men practice new forms of control as they simultaneously experience loss and are subjected to power imbalances in the United States. Gendered discourses are not "static ascriptions," but "story operators, ways of structuring relationships" (Haraway 1986: 85). While the specifics of gendered migrations may vary regionally throughout Mexico and within different global flows, a framework that prioritizes gender can be expanded to other cases, and many of the patterns outlined below may be present in different migration contexts (e.g., Dreby 2009; Smith 2006). Research that closely examines interactions between men and women can enrich our understandings of the lived experiences of male and female migrants.

Masculinity is both reconstituted and compromised by (im)migration to the United States, which in turn, simultaneously liberates and puts new controls on women, redefining femininity and what it means to be a woman.

Men are expected to migrate, and the masculinity of those who do not go north is called into question. Yet, men may have their masculinity stripped from them once they are in the United States, as they leave behind their role as farmers to work in low-wage jobs. Meanwhile, women who stay in Mexico face new burdens alongside increased freedoms: still responsible for domestic chores and child care, women take on tasks that were previously understood as the sphere of men, such as farming and managing finances. The lives of women living in the United States also transform—they are often in wage labor for the first time, and their roles in the family are notably altered. Rosa's assertion—"¡*Ya soy hombre y mujer!*/Now I am a man *and* a woman!"— underscores how gendered migrations are always gendered moves.

"If you don't go to the United States, you are not a man": Masculinities and the Shifting Status of Men

(Im)migration and transnational movement impact what it means to be a man, what is appropriate masculine behavior, and how men are judged in both sending and receiving communities. Indeed, even men who have never been to the United States are affected significantly by (im)migration and the individuals who do go. No longer able to support their families as they have in the past, men go to the United States to fulfill their role as providers, or stay in Mexico and are reminded of how their work in the *milpas* cannot financially maintain a household. Masculinized migration is driven by economic necessity. Essentially every male in the community is a farmer, but growing beans in arid land without irrigation is clearly difficult. During years of drought, there is no harvest, and even if rains do come, farmers are fortunate just to break even. In fact, even with the support of PROCAMPO—a program through the Mexican federal government that provides subsidies to rural farmers—it is difficult to cast this as subsistence farming. As one woman in the community told me, men migrate in order to support their farms in Mexico: a large portion of remittances go toward equipment, farmhands, and other expenses incurred in order to maintain their agricultural way of life. Increasingly, to be a man, one must migrate.

One afternoon in front of San Marcos' elementary school, Aída told me about her husband's experience with migration. Aída and Ramón married when they were twenty years old, and they lived in the home of Ramón's family. Aída was soon pregnant, and the young couple prepared to become parents. Meanwhile, Ramón's father, Gabriel, became increasingly concerned about Ramón's ability to support his wife and baby. Gabriel took Ramón aside and told him that the time had come for him to migrate to the United States to work and earn money for his new family. As Gabriel told Ramón: "*Si no vas a los Estados Unidos, no eres hombre* [If you don't go to the United States, you are not a man]." Ramón shared his plans with Aída, but she protested—she did not want him to go, especially with their first child arriving in just a few months. That same day, despite the fact that Aída was absolutely opposed to him going, Ramón left for the United States.

Aída said that the wishes of Ramón's father and cultural pressures to "be a man" by going to the other side were more powerful than his wife's desire for him to stay. "I thought that a good man was one who stands by his wife and children," she said. Today, four years later, Aída has a somewhat different perspective on her husband's migration. She said that she now realizes that her husband's trip to the north was necessary for their family, and the couple hopes that they will not be apart for much longer. Aída said that she and Ramón have been talking about the possibility of reuniting the family in New Mexico, though it will require saving a considerable sum of money to cover the cost of services of a *coyota*. When I asked Aída how her life would have been different had her husband never migrated, she said that she cannot imagine how they would have gotten by if Ramón had stayed. Despite the difficulties Aída has experienced since her husband left, Ramón's work in New Mexico is what provides for their family.

The centrality of migration in the construction of masculinity was also expressed at a wedding ceremony that joined Martín and Alejandra. On a warm, spring day, more than one hundred people were packed in the rancho's small chapel for the long-awaited event. The town's church is a one-room structure with a cross above its entrance. The ceremony was attended by primarily women and children—as well as the father and uncles of the bride—all dressed in their finest apparel.

The groom, Martín, had been in the United States for the past four years, sending money to Alejandra so they could build the home they would live in together. On this morning, after many years apart, the home was ready and the young couple was finally getting married. The priest talked about how Martín was a "good man," a hard worker who knew how to make sacrifices. In fact, explained the priest, he had already spent years in the United States earning money. Martín had shown that he could provide for his wife and that he would make an honorable husband. The priest's description of Martín was glowing—this marriage, he told family and friends, would grow and flourish.

After the ceremony, the wedding party and attendees formed a procession that followed a mariachi band through the streets of town to the home of

Martín's parents. There, the corral had been transformed into a festive reception site. In preparation for the event, family members had spent the entire week working—the men had killed a goat and roasted it over an open fire, while the women cooked in multiple kitchens simultaneously. Martín and Alejandra sat at the head table, flanked by a bubbling fountain and an enormous cake with red, whipped-cream roses. Several of Alejandra's uncles had traveled from California for the event, and they were waiting at the reception, their shiny SUVs parked in front of the house. People attending the wedding certainly took notice. Teen boys gathered longingly around the trucks, and several people mentioned that Alejandra's relatives had been very successful migrants. One woman said the uncles were just showing off, and that their wives and children—wearing expensive clothes—were aloof and uppity. Simultaneously evoking criticism, envy, and pride, these men were symbolic of migration for community members, representing a particular construction of manliness.

These cases demonstrate how the creation of masculinity is strongly tied to migration. While there are, of course, other spheres through which males express masculinity, transnational movement is a primary stage where expressions of male subjectivities are performed. Migration is a process that impacts virtually all men, those who migrate and those who do not. In this community, migration is equated with masculinity and calls it into question: if going to the United States is a primary path to manhood, there are profound implications for men who stay in Mexico.

Male identity in San Marcos and surrounding communities—which has been defined traditionally through working one's land and providing for one's family—is changing significantly. For men who do not migrate, masculinities are often expressed through exaggerated performances of manliness. While "real men" migrate, men who do not may need to prove themselves through hyperpresentations of male identity, arguably a kind of compensation for not fulfilling the expected role of migrating to financially support family. Men in Mexico often put on exaggerated displays of masculinity— including "jokes" about control over women, bouts of drinking, violence against partners and children, fights with other men, and even shootings—in large part because their manhood is threatened.

Violence as a presentation of masculinity takes multiple forms, against women and against other men. In hushed voices, women have told me of beatings from fathers and husbands, and although I have not witnessed violent acts between partners, I have seen the repercussions of these interactions. On one visit to the home of an extended family in the rancho, for example, I immediately sensed an atmosphere of tension and unease. When I had visited in the past, the matriarch of the household was one of the first to greet me. This day, however, she did not do so. Her adult daughter, Carina, greeted me, apologized profusely, and explained that her mother would be there shortly. There had been a disagreement, she whispered, between her parents and her father had hit her mother. Probably responding to my look of alarm, Carina assured me that everything would be fine. She approached the violence in a matter-of-fact way, asking, "But your husband hits you sometimes, doesn't he?" When I replied that, no, he never had, she responded with disbelief. After a few minutes, the *señora* appeared, and while she seemed distracted, she smiled and proceeded as if nothing was out of the ordinary.

An analysis of gendered violence in the community challenges essentializing representations of male aggression as naturally masculine or inherently Mexican (see Gutmann 1996). Such research uncovers the gendered character of "everyday" (Scheper-Hughes and Bourgois 2004: 2) or seemingly "ordinary" (Stewart 2001) violence while also contextualizing male power within cross-cultural perspective. The philosopher Uma Narayan argues that when Westerners consider intimate violence in countries throughout the world, there is a tendency to assume a direct connection between culture and violence but identify violence in Western nations—such as domestic violence in the United States and the exceptionally high rates of murder associated with it—as isolated acts by troubled individuals. Narayan terms this narrative "death by culture" (Narayan 1997: 81), presenting a discussion of Western perspectives on what have been labeled "dowry deaths" in India to reflect on the gendered character of violence in the United States and beyond. This frame can be useful to consider violence in (im)migrant communities, especially as such force extends and shifts transnationally. Gendered violence can intensify in the United States (see chap. 5) and takes on new forms against a backdrop of U.S. immigration policies.

Men, too, are subjected to violent acts, most often perpetuated by other men, and masculinity is often expressed through male–male violence. For many men, drinking can intensify such violence: drinking stints are frequent, and often continue for several consecutive days. For example, violence was at the center of one year's celebration of Mexico's Independence Day. Many (im)migrants had returned to the rancho to visit with family and friends and the town was filled with activity; residents went from home to home, sharing meals and catching up with those who had been away for extended periods. After the rodeo ended, a large group of people, primarily men, gathered together leaning against their trucks, laughing, and drinking. Suddenly, a crowd formed in one corner to watch a fistfight between an uncle and his nephew. The argument took an especially violent turn when the uncle pulled out a gun. The festivities ended abruptly with a drunk and angry man waving his gun in the air while community members ran to their homes for cover.

Exaggerated displays of manliness are not new, nor are they limited to the rancho: such masculinities are also presented across the border though the motivations behind these performances are often distinct in the two countries. Because of widespread male migration and as a response to threatened masculinity, expressions of manhood have taken on renewed importance in Mexico. Transnational labor migration is a primary reason for such performances of masculinity. One woman's sarcastic comment to me, "Here, men work only eight days a year!"—referring to men's seasonal and intermittent work in the fields—underscores the decreasing status of men who do not migrate.

Changes in men's position are also underway in the United States. When men from the rancho go north, they often find employment in the service sector—typically busing tables, preparing food, or washing dishes at restaurants, and occasionally working in construction. This is a significant shift for men coming from rural Mexico, where they essentially work for themselves, managing their farms (Rouse 1992). Such changes result in a loss of autonomy and a kind of erosion of masculinity as it is defined in men's home communities. As men go from being farmers who work for themselves to laborers who work for others, they are stripped of their masculinity, and arguably, feminized (see Malkin, 2004: 79). This process results in particular performances of masculinities in the United States as well.

The experiences of Carlos, a man who has never migrated, uncovers layers of contradiction within expressions of masculinity. Carlos is among the minority in his rancho—he has never been to the United States (although his father, all of his brothers, and most of his male cousins have), and he does not intend to go anytime soon. He told me that he does not want to bother with migrating north and finding work in the United States. He said that his life in the rancho is fine, that he enjoys farming and the simplicity of rural living. He discussed everything that he perceived that he might have to give up by going to the United States, explaining that because of the laws on the other side he would not be able to enjoy himself by, for example, sitting in his truck and drinking beer with friends. Carlos' sentiments about not being permitted to drink alcohol in a vehicle suggest a larger narrative that males associate with migration: a loss of autonomy.

Migration enables a man to enact masculinity through labor that supports him and his family, and yet, as Carlos describes, migrating to the United States is also equated with living under the control of the nation-state and being employed in low-wage, often exploitative service sector work—a particularly de-masculinizing endeavor and one that threatens male (patriarchal) power. Carlos' place within the global economy points to a further bind males face as they assert and attempt to maintain masculinities: the loss of autonomy that Carlos keenly associates with migration is hardly remedied by staying in Mexico. There, Carlos is unable to sustain his family through his work as a farmer; he is dependent on his brothers' remittances. In fact, Carlos' wife, Magdalena, told me that she pressures him constantly to join his father and brothers in order to work in the United States. She recently gave him an ultimatum: find employment in Mexico that actually earns money or head north. Males face this bind in maintaining and constructing masculinities. Men who do not migrate are unable to adequately support their families, a reality that brings shame to them and their partners, children, and extended family members.

This dilemma—to stay or to go—is not easily resolved. While most males do migrate, all males, whether they are in San Marcos, Dallas, Albuquerque, or elsewhere, are subject to the constraints inherent in the workings of capital. The critical narratives presented by migrants about their place in the global order reflect this and have a decidedly gendered dimension. Typically, male migrants present narratives that speak to the nexus of class and race while female migrants articulate critiques that emphasize gender. For example, several individuals from San Marcos work at the same manufacturing plant in the United States. The males who work there frequently talk in a disparaging way about their manager, a white, middle-aged man whom they call, "*El Pelón*," a nickname meaning "Baldy." The men who work for *El Pelón* constantly make jokes about his appearance (especially referring to the fact that he is white and overweight), or what *El Pelón* said, ate, or did on any given day. This discourse serves as commentary on the men's position as racialized and gendered laborers, a kind of reassertion or salvaging of masculinity in a context that threatens it. Interestingly, women at the same workplace rarely engage in this kind of banter. In fact, when it starts up, they often use it as an opportunity to poke fun at their husbands, brothers, and cousins, generally by rolling their eyes and smirking at one another. Women also experience a loss of autonomy through wage labor, but as described in the following section, their experiences and the focus of their social critiques are quite different from those of men.

Although masculinity is closely associated with migration, many men discover a disconnect when they actually do migrate. Rather than experiencing migration as an empowering process, men are often disappointed when they arrive in the United States and respond with new performances of masculinity. For example, Andrés first came to Albuquerque when he was seventeen. In his hometown in Mexico, Andrés was popular and socialized often, attending dances, dating women, and drinking with his friends. Young women in the rancho characterized Andrés as a very eligible bachelor; he was handsome and charming, and because most of his siblings had migrated to the United States, it was likely that Andrés would as well. When Andrés arrived in Albuquerque, however, he found that life in *el norte* was quite different than he had imagined. He worked long hours, and went from being a leader among his peers to one member of a community of migrants just trying to get by. Andrés borrowed a large sum of money to purchase a truck and went even further in debt by attending expensive concerts and events at local night clubs. Family members were very concerned about Andrés, especially when he started to have run-ins with the police. He was arrested twice, once for fighting with a man at a bar and once for reckless driving. For Andrés, expressions of masculinity took on new meanings after he had migrated.

The case of Félix provides another example of the multiple "meanings of macho" (Gutmann 1996) and the range of potential "masculinities" that may be expressed or enacted. Félix first came to the United States in the early 1980s. He would come seasonally, working in agriculture in Texas and Washington State. Since he was undocumented, each crossing into Texas was uncertain, and yet he did so numerous times. Eventually, he was able to establish U.S. permanent residency through IRCA, the Immigration Reform and Control Act. But despite his legal status, Félix has chosen not to settle in the United States. Although he could begin the process of applying for residency for his family, his wife and three children still live in their home in the rancho. Félix often makes the trip north to New Mexico to work at odd jobs, but he frequently returns to Mexico. He makes sure that he is in Mexico several times a year—to meet with PROCAMPO representatives each spring, to plant beans in the summer, and to harvest them in the fall.

Félix's identity as a man is strikingly distinct when he is in Mexico and when he is in the States, and his experience illustrates the dramatically different positions of men in Mexico and the United States. Félix told me that he is unwilling to bring his family to the United States because he does not approve of many "American" ideals, and he does not want his children raised here. And while this is a concern shared by many transnational Mexicans, Félix also seems to recognize his tenuous masculinity in the United States. Whether it is his specific intention or not, by maintaining his life in Mexico, he is protecting his power within the family, his status within the community, and ultimately his identity as a Mexican man. While Félix uses his legal status to protect his masculinity within Mexico, men's documented status can also redefine and reshape masculinity in the United States. Since masculinity is often equated with migration, one result is that male identity intersects with legal status within the United States. Men with U.S. citizenship or U.S. permanent residency are more powerful—and therefore seen as more masculine—than their counterparts who are undocumented.

Enrique also exemplifies these emergent formations of masculinity linked to U.S. legal status among transnationals. Although he has four brothers, Enrique was the first to naturalize as a U.S. citizen, and so he is the de facto patriarch of his transnational family. Since several of his siblings are undocumented, Enrique is responsible for many of the duties that other male family members are unable to carry out because of their insecure position within the United States. Enrique is currently petitioning for family members to acquire residency, including his parents and several siblings. He works in a higher paying job than many others from the rancho, and he was recently promoted to an assistant manager position. He is able to travel back and forth between Mexico and the United States easily—and for less money since he does not have to hire a *coyote*—and so it is Enrique who travels to Mexico when there is a sick relative or help needed on the family farm. In the United States, Enrique frequently meets family and friends at the border and facilitates their border crossings. He houses family and community members, and helps them find employment. He is well respected within the community as a successful migrant and as a good man.

This is a new form of masculinity that is being ushered in with transnational movement: paradoxically, a man is better able to provide for his family in Mexico when he has U.S. permanent residency or U.S. citizenship. A man with documents—unlike men who are undocumented—clearly has increased privilege within the United States. While there are some women who gain legal status in the United States, they almost always do so through their relationship with a male partner, or perhaps a father or brother, and so the power of "legalization" is closely linked to masculinity. It is primarily men who have been in a position to legalize their status first within the family because of the amnesty through IRCA. One's immigration status, and particularly "illegality," shapes gender relations and guides migrations (see chap. 5). Intersecting with the U.S. immigration status of men and women, power is redistributed according to an already well-established gender hierarchy, one in which male power is strong and pervasive.

"I do everything!": Women's Changing Roles

The reassertion of male power does not mean, however, that changes are not occurring among women—indeed, the place of women is also undergoing significant transformation because of (im)migration. With large numbers of men away in the United States, women, who were once responsible for exclusively domestic work, are increasingly taking on roles that were previously performed by men, such as attending school meetings, managing household finances, supervising labor in the family farm, and overseeing home construction and renovation projects (see also Pribilsky 2004, 2007). The growing number of female-headed households in the rancho are resulting in emergent constructions of womanhood. As men (im)migrate to the United States, they must relinquish some of their power within the family; men, however, do not easily let go of control over their wives and children. New forms of gender relations and subjectivities surface, and challenge previous ideals of what it means to be a woman.

Consider Celia, a woman in her late twenties with two young sons. Celia's husband, Miguel, has been in the United States for more than three years. She lives in the rancho with her sons, ages three and five. Celia and Miguel's house is one of the newer houses in the community. Celia proudly took me on a tour of her home, pointing out the bathroom, her new bedroom set, a microwave oven, and a Nintendo video game system, all improvements or purchases funded through remittances her husband sends regularly. In Miguel's absence, Celia is responsible for their home and family. "I do everything!" she told me. "Without my husband, I do it all."

Celia's day-to-day life is vastly different from that of women of the previous generation or that of her neighbors whose husbands have not migrated. She has notable independence: she owns a truck that she drives to neighboring towns for family visits or to Zacatecas in order to withdraw money that Miguel sends for the family. She manages the family finances and oversees her sons' schooling. For several years she supervised the building of her family's home—selecting and purchasing supplies, as well as locating, directing, and paying laborers. Celia said that she and Miguel speak by telephone often, and although Celia does consult with her husband about important family decisions, she recognizes her increased autonomy. She explained, "My life changes when Miguel is *here.*" Celia told me that when her husband is in the rancho he expects her to work constantly: she has to wake up early to clean the house and prepare elaborate meals. Celia said that when she is alone she lightens up on domestic chores—for example, she prepares simple food for her sons, and if she doesn't feel like making the bed, she will not do so.

Some women on the rancho are experiencing more independence than ever before. With their husbands in the United States, women are now responsible for a wide range of roles. Femininities are in flux: today, there are multiple ways to be a woman. But these new expressions of femininity are often contested, and women face challenges as they create new gender subjectivities, underscoring a misalignment between the condition (collective history) and situation (particular circumstances) of women (Lagarde y de los Rios 2003). Rosa's announcement that she was now "a man *and* a woman" must be contextualized within the previously rigid gender roles in her community and significant power imbalances between the sexes that—despite rapid change—persist today. The shift in the position of women collectively, as well as the situations of individuals, is a complex negotiation involving both the erosion and the reconstitution of male power.

According to some feminists, women's expanding roles lead to new freedoms (see discussion in Pessar 1999). Certainly, growing responsibility within the family is changing the place of females vis-à-vis males and within the community as a whole, but it is unclear to what extent women are liberated as a result of migration. As women gain independence, they are also facing new struggles and newly configured male power. The "double day" takes on new meaning as women are responsible for a range of gender roles. As one woman told me, it is very difficult to be "*una mujer sola* [a woman on her own]" in the rancho. In addition to the stress of increased responsibilities, women face further challenges: newly constituted male dominance and gendered power inequalities, domestic violence, and in many cases, abandonment by their husbands.

When I spoke with Cristina, a woman living on the rancho, about changes she has seen in families because of migration, she explained that men still control, or attempt to control, their wives from thousands of miles away. Husbands maintain a type of long-distance or transnational male dominance through male family members, budget management, phone calls, threats, and "*chismes* [gossip]" (see also Bever 2002; Dreby 2009; Mahler 2001). Cristina said that men often "*manden desde allá* [control from afar]"—they may ask a son or brother to step in as a surrogate head-of-household, or husbands may telephone incessantly and question wives about their whereabouts. Men also solicit the assistance of other men in town to keep an eye on their partners and to report to them about what female family members have been doing. Finally, men exert control by not sending money for family support or by threatening to abandon their wives for another woman—a threat that is actualized in many partnerships.

Mexican women living in the United States are also subjected to emergent formations of male control, and often they, too, do not find themselves "liberated" in the ways that some theorists might speculate. Once women have come north, they again live under the daily control of a male head-of-household, more so than those women who are living in Mexico. Additionally, like women in Mexico, women in the United States take on growing workloads, now in the sphere of wage labor as well as in the home. Rather than freeing women, work outside the home can be an increased burden, particularly because men are not compensating by taking on more of what has previously been labeled "women's work." Finally, migration disrupts strong female networks; groups of friends and family members play a central role in the daily lives of women in Mexico but such support can be difficult to sustain in the United States (see also Stephen 2007: 207).

When women (im)migrate to the United States, they may find themselves under the watch of men as they were not in Mexico. Most of the time, they migrate with males, and then live with boyfriends or husbands or perhaps brothers and other male relatives. It is very rare for women to migrate alone and even more so for them to live on their own once they have arrived. In the United States, men continue to have significant control over women's actions. Such findings complicate notions that migrations inevitably lead to gender egalitarianism. If men with legal status in the United States embody emergent masculinities and new forms of male power, women who are undocumented are perhaps the most vulnerable, underscoring the importance of considering the gendered aspects of "illegality" in the United States.

The experiences of Lupe illustrate this point. Lupe lived in San Marcos for several years while her husband, Antonio, was working and living in Albuquerque. When it became clear that Antonio, who is undocumented, would not be returning to the rancho anytime soon, he arranged for a *coyota* to bring Lupe and their three youngest children to New Mexico. In San Marcos, I met Lupe when she was living without her husband. Community members characterized Lupe as an opinionated, somewhat feisty woman who did not acquiesce to others. While I was in Mexico conducting field research, Lupe was often the focus of complaints from her neighbors—she always played music loudly from her house, people said, and without her husband in town she seemed to have license to do whatever she wished.

When I visited Lupe in Albuquerque, however, I was struck by the dramatic change in her demeanor and way of life. After migrating without documents, she was living in what was previously an all-male apartment where she was expected to cook and clean for not only her husband but also for her brother-in-law and two other men from the rancho. She told me that she felt very lonely, that she hardly ever left the house, and that she very much missed Mexico. Like Lupe's husband, men often bring women to care for them and perform domestic duties, and as a result, previous forms of masculinity are reasserted. In fact, one of the motivations for men to reunite their families in the United States is that men are able to reestablish themselves as head-of-household, and take advantage of the privilege that comes with the position.

It is common for women, like Lupe, to be isolated in the United States, especially when they first arrive. Another example is Esperanza, a woman who migrated with her husband and children. She had been in Albuquerque for eight months when she described her life in the United States to me. She said it was quite different than she had imagined. Because she was taking care of her children and the children of a cousin full time, she hardly left the house. Esperanza told me that she longed for the opportunity to go out, but since her husband worked during the weekend, it was difficult. When her husband was not working, he did not hesitate to go out drinking with other men from the rancho. Esperanza said that it was very frustrating to have her husband out drinking until the early morning hours, but that her pleas with him to stay home seemed futile.

Still, women do not passively submit to new forms of male control and exaggerated performances of masculinity. Instead, they challenge such demonstrations of power, especially through well-articulated critiques of men. For example, one evening while I was talking with Victoria in the rancho, her brother-in-law Santiago walked in. He smelled of alcohol, his eyes were glazy, and he was slurring his words. Santiago said he would not be coming to the English classes I taught each week. He explained that he had never attended school and did not know how to read or write, although, he assured us repeatedly, "I am very intelligent." As he spoke, Victoria and her mother looked at one another and then at me, smirking. Finally, Victoria, clearly irritated, responded: "In my opinion, it is not intelligent to be drunk every day." Santiago pretended to ignore her shaming comment, although he quickly left the room.

In kitchens, at family celebrations, or on shopping trips, women provide their own assessment of the workings of power in their lives. One evening in San Marcos, a group of primarily women met to play *lotería*, a game similar to bingo but played on cards covered with vivid images. The group had agreed that the cost to play would be one peso for each card, and some of the participants took the game quite seriously, arriving with plastic bags weighed down with coins ready for bidding. As the hostess called out the cards she drew, "*La Sirena . . . El Mundo . . . La Palma*," the players talked, joked, and laughed. I asked one woman, Honoria, if her husband had been to the United States, "*¡Sí, conoce los Estados Unidos, y mucho más!* [Yes, he knows the United States, and much more!]" Everyone laughed out loud, and then Honoria explained to me that her husband was with other women when he was in Dallas. She said that her husband continues to deny his extramarital relationships, but that several people from the rancho, including her cousins and a sister-in-law, told her that her husband was unfaithful. Through humor, Honoria expressed her disapproval of her husband's behavior.

While many male discourses provide commentary about their place in the economic order—such as jokes about *El Pelón*—women's critical narratives tend to focus on men and the gendered relations that shape their lives. Although females, like males, experience marginalization as laborers, it is women's everyday relations with men—their employers, but particularly their partners, fathers, brothers, uncles, and cousins—that are especially salient. It is the daily interactions between males and females—these gendered moves—that are often primary in women's lives.

Some of the strongest critiques from women are expressed through humor at all-female gatherings. I have attended events in both countries in which women presented candid commentary about male control. In these settings, jokes center on a reversal of gendered and often sexual power and/or the deflation of male domination. For example, at a *despedida* [farewell party] organized by mothers at the elementary school, women played a game that involved tying a pencil to a string that was then fastened around their waists so that the pencil hung down between their legs. The object of the game was to be the first woman to lower the pencil into one of the soda bottles on the ground. As women squatted up and down and moved their hips back and forth, the audience squealed, hooted, and cheered. Similarly, at a baby shower in the United States, there was a constant stream of sexual jokes, most of which described an extremely large phallus, not as a symbol of power but as a source of embarrassment for men. Reflecting overlapping regimes of power, women told numerous tales of President Bill Clinton and the sexual adventures—typically recounted as failings—of that powerful world leader. Far from enacting the stereotype of the submissive, modest Mexican woman, female (im)migrants present well-articulated critiques of gendered and national hierarchies through humor that underscores and aims to undermine male power.

Males (re)create and (re)assert masculinities in the United States and women who migrate face new and persistent forms of male control. Through migration, however, women do exercise flexible and diverse roles and redefine what it means to be a woman, even as they are subjected to ongoing male dominance. Teresa, for example, has a life quite distinct from her previous life in Mexico. In Mexico, she was constantly in her home doing domestic chores, and her family struggled because they had so little money. Today, Teresa works full time for a cleaning business, and she is responsible for many public interactions—with her children's teachers and doctors, the family's immigration attorney, bank tellers, and her realtor, among others. But while Teresa finds herself in spheres that are entirely new for her, and in charge of important family business, she still is the one who must do everything in the home. Her teenage daughters help with the load, but her husband and son do not.

Teresa tells me that she is exhausted. When she talks about her work, she describes it as yet another burden in her life, one that is heaped onto her many other responsibilities. Teresa portrays her work for the cleaning service as an undesirable necessity since she and her husband are saving money to buy a house; some migrants even portrayed women's work outside the home as "shameful," especially for men. With exasperation, Teresa says that she has purchased a daily planner—something she thought was ridiculous when she first saw a co-worker using one. But now, she explains, her life is so hectic that she is lucky to just get by. Although she knows it is unlikely, and still vividly recalls the difficulties she faced as a woman before coming to the United States, Teresa often dreams of returning to Mexico.

Migration scholars have argued that global migrations can lead to more balanced power relations between men and women, especially through women's work outside the home and the resulting power within partnerships and families (e.g., Hirsch 2003; Hondagneu-Sotelo 1994; Levitt 2001; Grasmuck and Pessar 1991; Stephen 2007). My research has similarly uncovered ways in which women's changing roles push the boundaries of gender ideologies. The ethnographic study of gendered moves can also emphasize changes that are taking place—and, importantly, not taking place—among men and the ways that migration fosters previous and new forms of male dominance and male privilege (see also Mahler 2001). The reconstitution of male power can surface in multiple forms, some more virulent than others.

Cristina told me that men continue to valorize agricultural work while diminishing the importance of work done by women. She explained that today women do both "women's work" and "men's work," and she asked, "Why can't men help with cleaning and caring for the children?" Such changes to male lifestyles are very slowly coming about in the rancho and perhaps only slightly more so in the United States. For example, when men live in all-male apartments in the United States, they will take turns cooking for one another, and some (typically younger) women in Mexico scoff when their migrant husbands return to the rancho and expect to be waited on; men essentially never cook when they return to Mexico or if their wives join them in the United States. In fact, the experiences of Teresa are common among women engaged in wage labor in the United States: women continue to be responsible for nearly all domestic tasks, even with full-time work schedules. Although women are challenging gendered norms and reshaping gender subjectivities, it seems unlikely that gender parity will emerge from within multiple systems that perpetuate such strongly gendered relations of power.

The preparation of tortillas is a way to gauge a male partner's control over, or attempts to control, his spouse. The following vignettes demonstrate the nuanced ways that gender relations and subjectivities are performed within transnational migration, and underscore the shifting context within which males and females interact. Consider the diverse experiences of three women—Marta, Piedad, and Teresa. Both Marta and Piedad stayed in the rancho while their husbands went to the United States, and both women's spouses returned to Mexico during my fieldwork, while Teresa, mentioned earlier, was living with her husband in the United States throughout my research.

After Marta's husband had been in the rancho for about a month, I stopped by to visit. The times I had visited Marta when she was living without her spouse, she was cheerful and friendly. After her husband returned, her demeanor changed significantly. Her daughter greeted me at the door and brought me back to a small room with a dirt floor and an *horno* [wood-burning oven]. Marta was sitting over the *horno*, tending to the fire with perspiration dripping from her temples. She was rolling small balls of *maza*, patting the dough between her palms, and placing the fresh tortillas inside the oven. She was clearly tired and under stress. She apologized profusely, explaining that because of all the work she had to do, she would not be able to spend much time visiting. I was surprised to see her making tortillas because the majority of women in the rancho purchase tortillas, making them by hand only on special occasions and typically with groups of other women. I asked Marta if there was an upcoming event that had prompted her to make tortillas. She said that her husband had demanded she make them for him. When she suggested they buy tortillas at the local *tienda*, she explained, her husband had become enraged, and so she felt she had no option but to do as he wished.

I also visited Piedad in her home after her husband returned from a several-year stay in Dallas. Piedad is about ten years younger than Marta, and while Marta lived with her husband in the rancho for many years, Piedad and her partner have spent the majority of their marriage living in different countries. Piedad told me that she was looking forward to her husband's return, but she knew that he would have certain expectations when he was home. Soon after I arrived, Piedad served us a lunch of *sopa* and beans with hard, crispy tortillas that can be purchased in a box. As we ate, Piedad's husband joked that now that he was back, Piedad should be making corn tortillas rather buying boxes of them. "Don't you think so, Debbie?" he asked me, smiling. Piedad just laughed it off. "Forget it!" she exclaimed. "You won't see me making tortillas by hand!"

I visited Teresa on a fall weekday evening in her apartment in Albuquerque. When I arrived, Teresa had just completed a full day working. After Teresa's son greeted me at the door, Teresa called me back to the kitchen, where she was preparing food. "It is almost finished," she said. "You should join us for dinner." In a scene that was commonplace over the course of my research, Teresa began warming tortillas as her husband and children sat in the living room watching television. Although Teresa and her spouse both work full time, it is Teresa who warms the tortillas—and cooks, makes the beds, does the family's laundry, and carries out all other household chores that need to be completed. Teresa's work outside the home has not reduced her responsibilities within the household. In some ways, women living alone in ranchos after their husbands have migrated may have the most flexibility to challenge gender roles and present alternative female subjectivities, but when men return, those patterns easily revert to previous gender orders (see also Bever 2002: 224). The experiences of Marta, Piedad, and Teresa demonstrate the diversity in negotiations between male and female partners, and underscore that some form of male domination shapes virtually all gender interactions, albeit to varying degrees.

Like men, women face a gendered dilemma whether they are in Mexico or in the United States and whether they are living with or without male partners, fathers, or brothers. In this female conundrum, women are subjected to existing and emergent masculinities and patriarchies in both places and neither setting offers egalitarian gender relations. And yet, in the context of transnational migration, females do challenge male power, question rigid gender ideologies, and experience transformations in their everyday lives. The boundaries that limit their actions are not fixed, and transnational movement is reshaping gendered selves among both women and men.

Gender Shifts

Through the interplay of gendered migrations and gendered moves, notions of appropriate gender roles are shifting. Transnational movement, cultural ideologies, the workings of global capital, and the persistence of the nation-state are resulting in a range of new gendered subjectivities: emergent forms of male power and strategies through which women assert themselves, as well as newly defined masculinities and femininities. These are transitions that "happen unevenly, and often result in contradictory combinations of everyday practices" (Hondagneu-Sotelo 1994: 193). Gender is created through such processes: masculinity is both reasserted and compromised because of migration between Mexico and the United States, and this, in turn, simultaneously frees and constrains women.

Shifting gender subjectivities problematize conclusions from previous research on changing gender roles and transborder movement. While theorists have often understood migration to be a path toward gender equity, my research complicates such models, demonstrating the starts and stops, new manifestations of power imbalances between men and women as well as changes that provide alternatives to gendered expressions. Such findings also suggest that some of the most potent challenges to confining gender constructions will come from those who are marginalized. Males who do not migrate and do not easily fulfill notions of "a good Mexican man," and females who migrate often and who are criticized for transgressing community norms are well positioned to be key players in destabilizing rigid gender ideals and effecting change in their families and communities.

The anthropologist Gail Mummert (1994: 207) outlines that "changes do not flow in a unilínear fashion, as in an elegant model, from female subservience to emancipation." Similarly, there are indirect and often unpredictable steps toward gender equity (Bustamante and Sánchez Trujillo, n.d.). As gender dynamics change with transnational movement, women will increasingly call on men to do their part even while facing intensified or emergent male power moves. Similarly, men will exercise gendered power and control as they construct new forms of masculinity that support family and community members in the process of migration. The creation and reconstitution of gendered selves is a complex and uneven process characterized by control, contention, acceptance, contestation, and, always, negotiation.

The interplay of gendered migrations and gendered moves is altering notions of appropriate gender roles. Transnational movement, cultural ideologies, the workings of global capital, and the power of the state to categorize individuals are resulting in a range of new gendered subjectivities. Never static, gender subjectivities are constantly evolving and shifting through what transnational feminists have called the "interminable project of production and reproduction" (Alarcón, Kaplan, and Moallem, 1999: 8). Like transnational migration itself, gender identities are characterized by flexibility, movement, and transformation. Masculinities and femininities will continue to change with (im)migration as transnational Mexicans participate in the constant and complex negotiation of gendered migrations and gendered moves. Migrants' understandings of gender intersect with state power, directing migration in decidedly gendered ways.

5

Gendered Borderlands

"We were hiding in the bushes . . . it was the middle of the night. We were there for what seemed like hours, with border patrol helicopters circling overhead. I'll never forget that night." José was describing his first and only trip north. Like other men from his town, he had gone at a young age—he was nineteen at the time. He traveled with several men from the rancho, including a friend and two cousins. Now in his forties, José recalled the night that had been, as he stated, life-altering. The young men had gone by bus to Tijuana, and then, because they were unauthorized to enter the United States, hired a *coyote* to facilitate their border crossing. The *coyote* was part of a larger operation: José and his companions were joined with several other migrants from different states in Mexico, a group that numbered close to twenty—all men except one young woman who was migrating with her husband. "And then," José explained, "it happened."

I met José early on during my fieldwork and he and his wife had mentioned his migration, saying that it had not worked out, that a tragic event had taken place, but neither had shared details with me. Although I knew José and his family well, he had never spoken with me about it, until one day when he decided that he should. "As we lay on the ground, with spotlights around us, they raped her." José continued and then looked away. "It was a group of *coyotes*, or men the *coyotes* arranged to meet there, I can't be sure. What was especially difficult, the horror I will never forget, was her husband's situation . . . I was next to him the entire time, and there was nothing he could do, nothing I could do, nothing we could do. *La migra* [U.S. Border Patrol] was looking for us, and the *coyotes* had knives and guns. We had no option but to wait." The rape shaped José's migration trajectory. He did make it across and went to work at a taco stand in San Diego, living in an apartment above the restaurant with a group of young men like himself. But, José explained, after crossing the border he never felt secure in the United States, and so after about six months he returned to the rancho and did not go north again. "It was like a bad dream," he said. "But unfortunately it was real."

José's story underscores several aspects of the gendered character of unauthorized Mexican migration to the United States: how migration patterns and border crossings are gendered, and the risks and violence for both males and females—as well as the specifically gendered dangers—when crossing without documents. His story also illustrates the effect of U.S. immigration status and the construction of illegality on gender relations and gendered experience. State power and processes that categorize migrants as "illegal" play out in the gendered actions and interactions of transnational Mexicans' everyday lives. Spatial locations, whether or not one migrates, and physical movement within a transnational space are particularly gendered. Increasingly, gender shapes and is shaped by undocumented migration against a backdrop of intensifying immigration controls at the U.S.-Mexico border and within the United States.

My analysis bridges literature about the production of "illegality" (e.g., Chavez 2001, 2007, 2008; Coutin 2000, 2005, 2007; De Genova 2002, 2005b; Ngai 2004; Willen 2007) with scholarship that demonstrates the gendered character of transnational migration (e.g. Donato et al. 2006; Hondagneu-Sotelo 1994, 1999b, 2003b; Mahler and Pessar 2001b, 2006; Pessar 1999). A focused gender analysis uncovers the distinctly gendered logics of processes that define migrants as "legal" or "illegal." Similarly, a gendered examination of how states legally categorize immigrants adds to understandings of how gender and intersecting identities are entwined with migration flows. Gendered crossings and gendered locations within the borderlands are always "situated" (Lamphere, Ragoné, and Zavella 1997) and tied to the intersection of gender and U.S. immigration status.

State-structured, arguably state-directed, gendered crossings and patterns of migration intersect with transnational Mexicans' notions of gender, creating the milieu of gendered borderlands. Gendered spaces include the U.S.-Mexico border and the areas surrounding it, although the borderlands also extend to the many places where transnational Mexicans live that may be thousands of miles from the border, locations in both Mexico and the United States. The specifically gendered character of borderlands includes spaces shaped by both constraint and possibility, and demonstrate the restrictions and potential that depend on gender positionality.

Gendered crossings illustrate how unauthorized entry and migration, as well as the perils of undocumented crossings and movement, are gendered. The trappings and dangers of transnational migration are experienced by both men and women, albeit in specifically gendered ways: gendered power imbalances within global flows are present, persistent. How transnational subjects are categorized by the U.S. government, the status of being undocu-mented or defined as "illegal" by the U.S. state, plays out according to sub-jectivities of gender—a primary focus here—as well as age, class position, or status within the sending community, among others. The gendered trans-gressions of transnationality demonstrate how the state's presence config-ures, intensifies, and/or disrupts desire, (in)fidelity, and gendered violence.

Gendered power dynamics are strong, though never formulaic or pre-dictable. Within communities and vis-à-vis state regimes, gendered power relations are not, for example, guided solely by male domination; instead, gendered exchanges are more aptly understood as a series of layered negotia-tions between and among men and women, shaped by individuals' construc-tions of gender and state power. The presence of the U.S. state defines gen-der actions and interactions in significant ways. U.S. immigration controls and the U.S. state's categorization of migrants can produce new—or intensify existing—gendered power imbalances. Such findings underscore the risks and uncertainties of migrating without documents, for both women and men, though also, significantly, reveal their gendered character.

At the Borders

Not easily defined or delineated, the borderlands are characterized by incon-sistencies—a place of divisions and unions, as well as conflict and exchange. Scholars have explored the paradoxical character of the borderlands, iden-tifying how borders separate even as they bring together nations, cultures, sexes, linguistic groups, and classes (e.g., Alvarez 1995; Anzaldúa 1987; Clif-ford 1997; Kearney 1998; Limón 1998; Wilson and Donnan 1998): borders are "barriers and opportunities, often simultaneously" (Wilson and Donnan 1998: 22). Such contradictions within the borderlands and the gendered ten-sions that emerge from borderland encounters are central to my analysis. The U.S.-Mexico borderlands are certainly gendered (see Segura and Zavella 2007), with multiple actors—including, for example, migrants, state agents, law enforcement, tourists, maquila workers, business executives—operating with more or less constraint or possibility depending on one's position or location along axes of gender and intersecting aspects of the self.

The U.S.-Mexico border is a clearly delineated territorial and political division, as well as a series of overlapping "microborders" (Wilson and Don-nan 1998: 3) that create the U.S.-Mexico borderlands: indeed, "no other bor-der in the world exhibits the inequality of power, economics, and the human condition as does this one" (Alvarez 1995: 451). This "2000-mile boundary dividing two nation-states" (Alvarez 1995: 448)—established through war—is currently maintained through U.S. militarization and domination (Rosas 2007). Despite violence along this international boundary, the border is also a space characterized by movement and exchange. Each day, "border people" (Martínez 1994) move from south to north and north to south as migrants, tourists, and laborers. The borderlands are constructed, maintained, and challenged through "bilingual, bicultural, and binational oscillations" (Canclini 1995: 235) and are "a perpetual creation" (Vélez-Ibáñez 1996: 266). "Borderization" reaches far beyond the territorial boundary (Gómez-Peña 1996: 240). Theorists argue that in today's "New World Border" (Gómez-Peña 1996), we all live "border lives" (Bhabha 1994: 1) and "all cultures are border cultures" (Canclini 1995: 261).

Much of the conflict in the borderlands—"borders are always domains of contested power" (Wilson and Donnan 1998: 10)—is the product of power relations between two nation-states and the unequal status of nations within the global political economy. The U.S.-Mexico borderlands have had a long history of violence and power struggles, reaching back before either nation-state existed. Multiple conquests, war, and imperialism have constituted the border, shaping the U.S.-Mexico borderlands in profound ways: today's battle in the borderlands is fought within "a changing 'Anglo' capitalist political economy" (Limón 1994: 15) and transnational capital establishes neocolonial relationships (Miyoshi 1993). Such political-economic histories are the backdrop to contemporary gendered orders of power. Transnationalism reflects and embodies a particular type of borderland, one in which a profound imbalance of power—in relation to capital, according to political influence, and along lines of race/ethnicity, and gender—plays out in the everyday lives of individuals living within and across distinct nation-states.

Borderlands divide/connect different countries but also represent the clashes/encounters of cultures, genders, classes, ethnic and racial groups, and generations, among others: "Borders are set up to define the places that are safe and unsafe, to distinguish *us* from *them*" (Anzaldúa 1987: 3). Indeed, identities structure inequality and injustice, creating "fences" (Vélez-Ibáñez 1996: 5), and "fault lines" (Almaguer 1994) throughout the borderlands. Borderland metaphors underscore power imbalances and are aptly applied to encounters between men and women, among ethnic/racial groups, and within class hierarchies (Vila 2000, 2005). The "'bumping' process" (Vélez-Ibáñez 1996: 6) or "encounters" (Limón 1998) within the borderlands—can be a kind of "war . . . sometimes literal, sometimes only thinly metaphorical, always political and cultural" (Limón 1994: 15). Such symbolic expressions of borderland interactions underscore the inequalities within boundary crossings and frontier settings, highlighting that not all powerful borders are transnational.

The border has become a potent metaphor for the self. The writer and social theorist Gloria Anzaldúa outlines how the self is both fluid and fragmented, a contradictory configuration of interconnected dimensions of subjectivity, and how identities are shaped through conflict, difference, movement, and hybridization (Anzaldúa 1987). Describing the self as "*La encrucijada*/The Crossroads" (Anzaldúa 1987: 80), Anzaldúa asserts "a tolerance for contradictions, a tolerance for ambiguity" (Anzaldúa 1987: 79). Similarly, the performance artist Guillermo Gómez-Peña describes himself as "a fluid border-crosser, intellectual 'coyote,' and intercultural diplomat" (Gómez-Peña 1996: 1). Social theorists identify the link between identity and transborder movement (e.g., Clifford 1997; Gupta and Ferguson 1997b; Lavie and Swedenburg 1996; Malkki 1992; Rapport and Dawson 1998; Wilson and Donnan 1998). Describing "migrants of identity" (Rapport and Dawson 1998), and "geographies of identity" (Lavie and Swedenburg 1996; see also Yaeger 1996), scholars explore the shifting character of subjectivities and power relations in borderland spaces.

The border then—as social, political, and economic boundary, symbolic construct, metaphor for the self, geographic divide, and space of inequality— is prominent in the lives of transnational Mexicans, for both those who have crossed it and those who have not. Gendered borderlands extend far beyond the geographic boundary: U.S. state actions, those that take place far from migrant sending communities in Mexico play out in the gendered politics of migrants' lives, so that, for example, even those who have never been to the U.S.-Mexico border or have not lived in the United States as an undocumented migrant may feel the state's presence in significant ways. Militarization and violence at the border shape border crossings and the intimate exchanges of transnational migrants.

Gendered Crossings

"I can't wait to go!" Benito proclaimed, grinning broadly. Seventeen-year-old Benito was dressed up, about to drive to a *baile* in a nearby rancho—he was wearing a satin shirt, black pants, a belt buckle with a bucking bronco, and shiny black cowboy boots. His thick, dark hair was slicked into place, and the scent of aftershave was strong. As he leaned against his family's truck, Benito told me the plans for his first migration to the United States. "I leave for the border tomorrow with my cousins. We'll go to Juárez, and then on to Albuquerque. There are so many opportunities for me there . . . I'll have a good job in a restaurant, there are great clubs for listening to music, I may even buy a truck of my own." As we spoke, several of Benito's friends gathered behind him, nodding approvingly as he described the details of his trip north. "I am so excited. I know I won't be able to sleep at all tonight! Benito and his cousins (fourteen and sixteen years old) did leave for the border the next day, and after several unsuccessful attempts at crossing—wading across the river, jumping on a train headed north—the young men crossed with the services of a *coyote* recommended by a family member.

Se Van/Se Queden

Migration, as described earlier, is an inherently gendered process. Nearly all men in the community migrate, most often for the first time as teenagers, as José and Benito did. The migration of women of all ages—and especially adolescent females—is, by comparison, discouraged, restricted, and/or closely controlled. When women do go to the United States without documents, males are involved in nearly every detail of women's crossings. Husbands, fathers, brothers, uncles, and/or male cousins make decisions about the timing of women's migrations, determine the details of if, how, and with whom they will cross the border, and physically accompany women when they are able to do so. Women's migrations are rarely "autonomous" in the ways that men's are: women migrate to reunite with male partners or because they have been abandoned by their spouses and must go to provide for their children. In nearly every case, regardless of the motivations, women's migration is tightly controlled by male family members.

The gendered character of border crossings and migration processes begins at a young age, and the gendered divisions within transnational experiences are evident early on in the life cycle. These gendered crossings and migrations have implications related to the (in)security of migrant families (chap. 3), how gendered relationships are structured and enacted (chap. 4), and the focus here, positionality within power structures and the resulting geographic locations of migrants depending on multiple aspects of the self, especially gender and state-defined immigration status.

Consider the experiences of Delia, seventeen years old, like Benito, but in circumstances that are quite distinct from his. "I'm going to the United States," Delia told me one afternoon. "Even if I have to go *"como mojada"* [undocumented], I am determined to go." Delia and her mother, Luisa, were standing in front of their house, waiting for the bus to a neighboring town. They held brightly colored *bolsas*, bags they would fill with fruits, vegetables, and grocery staples at the market. As Delia spoke, Luisa shook her head—her face expressed deep concern. "Delia is very enthusiastic about migrating, but she doesn't see the dangers. The United States is a temptation for young people. It seems like a good life, but it is a hard life, a difficult life." Luisa went on to talk about the migration of her sixteen-year-old son, Rafael. Two years earlier, Rafael had gone to Dallas, Texas, without papers. Now he is homesick and wants to return to the rancho, but he must stay and work to pay for the *coyote* who crossed him. Depressed and lonely, Rafael calls his mother frequently. He works long hours and, after paying for monthly living expenses, has only a small amount of money to go toward the debt he owes for his passage to the United States. "Yes, it is a temptation," repeats Luisa. "And much too dangerous for my daughter—there are too many risks for a young, single woman to cross." As the bus pulled up, it was Delia who shook her head. "I'm going," she said. "I'm determined to go."

Against the backdrop of state power and violence—especially gendered violence—at the U.S.-Mexico border, social pressures mean that young women such as Delia are prevented from migrating, while young men, such as Benito and Delia's brother, Rafael, do go. As one woman in Mexico explained:

> It is different for men and women. In the case of men, if they have papers or if they don't have papers, they go [*se van*]. It doesn't matter, either way they migrate. For women, on the other hand, if they have papers—and very few do—they go, but if they don't have papers, they don't go . . . they stay [*se quedan*].

If a man goes without formal authorization, he is a "good man," but if a woman is an undocumented migrant, especially a young woman, "*¡qué vergüenza!* [what shame!]." This demonstrates the power of papers, or rather, how categories constructed and enforced by the U.S. state through documentation mediate the movement of women and men. Because it is so difficult for rural, working poor Mexicans to obtain permission to enter the United States "legally," the result is that men go while women stay. Men have more flexibility to migrate and to determine how they do so, are able to be in the liminal spaces of the borderlands more regularly than women, and, significantly, are transnational actors with a wider range of options.

In the case of undocumented Mexican migration, there are parallels between gendered access to geographic movement and gendered power or autonomy (e.g., Ong 1999; Tsing 1993). Women's disadvantage in relation to men within the sphere of "travel" reflects broader "gendered political disadvantages" (Tsing 1993: 128), while "family regimes . . . generally valorize mobile masculinity and localized femininity" (Ong 1999: 20). The notion of moving, traveling, migrating men and localized or even contained women is a frame that resonates among transnational Mexicans, although gendered migrations do not necessarily follow a monolithic or predictable pattern. Intersecting state and familial structures of power (Ong 1999) create a setting in which women are contained while men experience (relative) flexibility. This underscores the specifically gendered character of undocumented migrations, flows shaped by both constraint and possibility that depend on one's gender in shifting circumstances.

Por la tierra/Por la línea

"They will cross *por la línea*," explained Mauricio as he described the upcoming border crossing of his wife, Lidia, and their two daughters ages eleven and five ["*por la línea*" means literally "at the line" or at a formal entry point along the border]. After nearly four years apart, Mauricio decided to reunite his family in the United States. Mauricio and his eldest sons, who were working in Nevada without documents, saved money to finance the passage of Lidia and the girls. The cost at the time was about $9,000 for the three female family members. Mauricio hired a *coyota* to facilitate their border crossing: *coyotas* are trusted to cross women more often than male guides or *coyotes*. It was, as Mauricio emphasized, imperative that the crossing be "*por la línea*," at a border station using documents that were valid but belonged to someone else. Such crossings are typically employed in the migrations of women and young children, the elderly, and, tellingly, legally vulnerable men, such as men who have been previously deported. Mauricio and his sons, by comparison, had never crossed with a *coyote* "*por la línea*"; instead, their crossings had always taken place, with or without a *coyote*, "*por la tierra*" ["by land" though this term can describe any crossing that is not at a border station, such as wading across the river or on a train]."

The fact that men typically cross "*por la tierra*" while women cross "*por la línea*" captures how some of the broader gender ideologies within this transnational community intersect with state-enforced border controls (see also

Donato, Wagner, and Patterson 2008 and O'Leary 2009 for discussions of women's border crossings). Gendered crossings demonstrate how movement across the border and the geographic placements of men and women of different ages are guided by understandings of gender within the community, though also, significantly, the realities of a heavily militarized border and U.S. state-defined categories of immigration status. The gendered divides—*"se van"/"se quedan"* and *"por la tierra"/"por la línea"*—express how men have more flexibility vis-à-vis the U.S. state. Men can go north more often, at a younger age, and via routes typically closed to women; adult and adolescent men operate in ways that girls and women cannot.

The relative autonomy of men who migrate without documents, however, is partial, always mediated or limited by the U.S. state's construction of illegality. The border is, of course, a risk to all migrants crossing without documents, and the dangers of unauthorized transnational migration are experienced by both men and women, but in specifically gendered forms. Since those who are undocumented are constructed as noncitizens, "illegal immigrants," or "aliens," their safety is not understood as the responsibility of the U.S. state; instead, state control of the border is framed as a method for protecting those with formal U.S. membership. Violence and insecurity at the border are perceived as coming from outside the nation, even when perpetuated by the state itself, through state actions and policies (e.g., Cornelius 2006; Heyman 1999a, 1999b). The border—a definitively legal construct on the part of the state—is also an extralegal space where, paradoxically, "illegal" practices take place (e.g., Heyman 1999c).

It is this insecurity at the border that shapes violence, gendered violence, and many of the gendered dimensions of migration. Border insecurities are carried out by agents of the state (such as border patrol officers), actors operating outside of the state (including other undocumented migrants or *coyotes*), as well as U.S. vigilantes who curiously frame their actions as "within the law to support enforcement of the law" (Minuteman Project 2009). The militarization, violence, and simultaneous lawlessness and intensive emphasis on the law at the border make it a place that is understood and experienced by transnational Mexicans as dangerous for all migrants, males and females of all ages. However, it is especially so for those disadvantaged by gender, age, and generation: very young children, the elderly, and particularly, women and girls. The militarized border extends far beyond the territorial boundary, dividing couples and affecting intimate relations, even when partners live thousands of miles from the border itself.

Gendered Transgressions

One fall afternoon, Petra, a young woman originally from San Marcos, left her home in Albuquerque with her infant son. After living in the United States for several years without documents, Petra and her son, a U.S. citizen, boarded a bus headed for Mexico. Petra was emotionally drained from months of fighting with her husband, Arturo, tired of his nights out drinking, and, especially, scared of his anger and increasing violence. She decided to take action and returned to San Marcos, the town she and her husband had left years before to find work. Because both Petra and her husband are undocumented, she knew it would be nearly impossible for him to take any legal action to gain custody of his son from within the United States, and that it would be difficult for him to follow her to Mexico since return back to the United States would be costly and dangerous.

Acting both within and outside of state power, Petra migrated from north to south as a strategy to flee an unhappy marriage and to protect herself and her son from violence. Her transnational movement empowered her in particular ways: her migration denied Arturo access to their son and secured her own separation from her husband. Above all, however, Petra's movement reflects gendered vulnerabilities. Petra's migration had followed an established pattern: she spent a period alone in Mexico, while Arturo was in the United States, and when she did migrate, Petra lived with Arturo, disconnected from female support networks she had in Mexico. Both Petra and Arturo are constrained by state power: they are unable to easily travel between Mexico and the United States, and their transnational lives are without question precarious, especially because of the ever-present threat of deportation. However, Petra's predicament in the United States was compounded by her husband's control within their relationship.

Although both Arturo and Petra are undocumented, gendered politics mean that Arturo exercises relatively more—albeit not absolute—power than Petra within the United States. Petra, as an undocumented migrant in the United States, did not feel secure engaging law enforcement in hopes of protection from violence. When Petra left the United States with her son, she was attempting to harness state power to challenge male domination, while Arturo's situation underscores the profound ways that the state restricts both males and females. The experiences of Arturo and Petra show how state power impacts gendered actors within families distinctly at different junctures.

State power is evident, and specifically gendered, in the physical migrations and border crossings of men and women. Additionally, the U.S. state's presence—through migration controls and categories of immigration status—plays out within transnational partnerships in specifically gendered ways. State authority and to some extent, the limits of the state, are simultaneously evident within binational relationships; state controls can, along lines of gender, facilitate or discourage migration, protect migrants from or expose them to violence, and disadvantage different individuals at different times. Thus transnational couples face state authority and employ strategies as they negotiate gendered partnerships. For transnational Mexicans, while men and women operate outside of state structures when they are able, state power intensifies gendered exchanges. As theorized by scholars of the borderlands, transnational spaces are characterized by contradictions, reflected in the paradoxical nature of gendered actions and interactions. These disjunctures often surface as gendered transgressions that are experienced within intimate relationships, yet always in the shadow of state power.

Transnational partnerships are the norm for Mexican migrants and, like geographic borders, such unions are characterized by ties and divisions, enduring or disintegrating over time and distance. Marriages and unions across and severed by the U.S.-Mexico border can take various forms, though relationships are shaped by a pervasive, normative heterosexuality (see Cantú 2009): a partnership may be civilly and/or religiously recognized, a common law union in which both partners and community members refer to the couple as "*esposos*/spouses," a relationship between a "*novio*/boyfriend or fiancé" and a "*novia*/girlfriend or fiancée," an extramarital partnership, or a second marriage with or without a partner's knowledge (for more on unions and sexual relations among transnational Mexicans, see González-López 2005; Hirsch 2003). Relationships are built across, and divided by, the international boundary: people meet and establish unions because of transnational movement, while migrants also understand conflicts, infidelities, separations, and divorces as stemming from migration. Transnational marriages and unraveling unions can be both the product of, and the motivating reason for, migration across the U.S.-Mexico border.

Consider another severed transnational tie, the case of Alicia and Gustavo. Gustavo was living and working in the United States without documents. Alicia was pregnant with their first child and living in the rancho. Gustavo and Alicia could no longer tolerate being separated, so Gustavo decided that Alicia should make the trip north. In keeping with the gendered patterns of border crossings, Gustavo arranged for a *coyota* to bring Alicia to the United States "*por la línea*." Soon after her arrival, however, Gustavo and Alicia began fighting, and Gustavo was often violent. One night, after

Gustavo had been out drinking with friends, he brutally beat his wife. Alicia, as an undocumented woman, was in a particularly vulnerable position vis-à-vis her husband, and yet, she strategically acted within a transnational space. Alicia, following the counsel of her sisters, called the police. She hoped that an arrest, given Gustavo's undocumented status, would ultimately lead to his deportation, and she was right. Gustavo spent two weeks detained and then was sent back to Mexico. After his return to San Marcos, Gustavo called Alicia repeatedly, begging her to join him. But Alicia refused—she remained in the United States, and several months later gave birth to their daughter, Olivia, a U.S. citizen. Alicia used the border and the U.S. legal system, manifestations of the state, to increase her own power in the gendered negotiations of her marriage. She strategically acted, albeit in limited ways, within a transnational space.

Similarly, in the lives of another young couple, Miguel and Violeta, gendered violence and individual reactions to the violence reveal the complicated terrain of gendered power within transnational partnerships. When Miguel became violent and struck Violeta, she called the police, and then took the couple's toddler and went to California to be with her sisters. Miguel "fled" as well, following Violeta. The couple later reconciled, but after a year Miguel was stopped for a traffic violation and deported to Mexico. Although Violeta and the child joined Miguel in Mexico, and the family is once again living together, Miguel's parents continue to blame Violeta for Miguel's return, alleging that police had a record of Violeta's call and, for this reason, deported Miguel. While the reality is that once apprehended, Miguel's deportation was nearly certain because of his undocumented status, Violeta continues to be at fault in the eyes of her in-laws. All three of the women described above, Petra, Alicia, and Violeta, fled situations of violence, but there continue to be gendered consequences and vulnerabilities in these women's lives.

Recognizing "the complexity and embeddedness of gender oppression" (Villalón 2010: 8), I situate gendered violence against a backdrop of the U.S. state's production of illegality. Here, direct violence against women is not (typically) perpetuated by the state; rather such violence is tolerated or exacerbated specifically because of U.S. immigration policies, making women vulnerable as they migrate transnationally (Menjívar and Salcido 2002; Salcido and Adelman 2004; Villalón 2010). While rates of domestic violence are not higher within immigrant communities in the United States, women's "situations are often exacerbated by their specific position as immigrants" (Menjívar and Salcido 2002: 898). Although the United States has implemented laws—such as the Violence Against Women Act (VAWA) and the Victims of Trafficking and Violence Protection Act (VTVPA)—which were created to protect (im)migrant women regardless of immigration status, in practice profound inequalities and what the sociologist Roberta Villalón calls formal and informal "barriers to citizenship" (Villalón 2010: 41, 79) persist.

Still, while gendered transgressions illuminate the transnational character of violence and show that violence is certainly gendered, such interactions also reinforce the fact that the specifics and consequences of violence are never entirely predictable. Intimate exchanges between partners instead demonstrate Mexican nationals' place—and in particular their vulnerability—within the United States. In the lives of each of these couples, individuals had more or less power and were directly or indirectly supported or abandoned by the U.S. state, at particular moments and within different situations. Although women sometimes used their partners' undocumented status in an attempt to protect themselves, violence and its effects continue outside of formal or "legal" structures and underscore the vulnerability of all undocumented migrants. As one mother, concerned for her son living without documents in the United States, told me, "*Los mojados no tienen derechos allá*/Undocumented immigrants don't have rights in the United States." Knowing how transnational individuals can be marginalized within the United States, and recognizing the decidedly gendered character of power relations between partners and within families, transnational Mexicans make choices and take action within the constraints of living without documents in *el norte*.

While undocumented migrants, both women and men, have little structural power, women living in Mexico whose partnerships end because of their husbands' infidelities with women in the United States are particularly disempowered.[1] All interpersonal relationships have difficulties and challenges, and, certainly, separations and infidelities are not only due to migration. At the same time, however, distance, extended time apart, and the pressures of migrating and living in the United States without documents puts considerable strain on relationships, resulting in different forms of transnational infidelities. Fractured relationships have a gendered character—indeed, gendered transgressions must be considered against the backdrop of "illegality" in the United States and its effects. One such gendered infidelity occurred between Gilberto and Camila. Camila attended English classes in San Marcos. She was quiet in class and very shy outside of the classroom, even around other people from the rancho. Camila had told me that her husband was living in Sacramento, and that she wanted to learn English because she hoped to join him there at some point in the future. One afternoon, Camila did not show up to class. The other students told me that Gilberto had called to tell

Camila that their marriage was over. Friends relayed that Camila was devastated. Camila did not return to the English classes, and when I saw her later, she made small talk but never again mentioned her husband or any desire to go to the United States.

Divergent notions of "fidelity" reveal the gendered character of transnational intimacies. Consider a conversation I had about infidelity with a woman in the rancho. "*Anda con otra* [He is with another woman]," said Lita, as she discussed the husband of her friend Zoila. "He has another partner in Texas, another life on the other side. But what can Zoila do? *Así es la vida* [That's how life is] . . . if it wasn't this woman, it would be another. There is always another woman." I have repeatedly heard this phrase, "*Anda con otra*"—as a statement of fact, as a declaration of injustice, as a personal lament. I have come to understand women's depictions of infidelities as telling reflections of gendered intimacies and sociopolitical exchanges.

When I first spoke with Zoila about her husband's infidelity, she initially joked about it, blaming the "*gringas*" for tempting Mexican men in the north. But in later conversations with Zoila and other women in the rancho, they expressed disappointment in men's disloyalties. In almost every case, it is husbands who have extramarital affairs, while wives are rarely unfaithful—a product of the thick layers of marginalization that women experience. Men, at every stage of migration, even when they are unauthorized to be in the United States, exercise more power and autonomy than women do. When men go north, family members keep a very close eye on female partners. Additionally, women are in a much more precarious position than men should infidelity occur. For example, a wife's infidelity—extremely unlikely in the first place—would not put a man in an economically vulnerable position. In fact, in one of the rare cases in which a woman slept with a man in the rancho while her husband was in the United States, her husband immediately cut her off financially, providing no support for her and their four young children. And, although Petra met a man after returning to Mexico, he refused to financially support Arturo's child, which again placed Petra in an economically and emotionally vulnerable situation.

Over the months following my conversations with Lita and Zoila, I learned that much of the frustration with Zoila's husband's infidelity—and male infidelity more generally—had to do with money: Zoila's husband was not supporting his family, and this was viewed as a profound injustice by Zoila and other women in the community. Recognizing "marriage as economic partnership" (Rebhun 1999: 118), women identify different forms of loyalty, and from their perspective infidelity is not solely or primarily linked to sexual transgression. Equally prominent, and in some circumstances more serious, are the infidelities that breach financial relations and responsibilities. While sexual infidelities can be forgiven, economic disloyalty has a lasting effect in the lives of a couple or family. This fidelity is often expressed as financial loyalty, rather than romantic or sexual devotion. As one woman described, "Really, what does it matter if my husband had an affair? Where is he now? He is with us, his family. He always sent money, all those years he was gone. I don't think he was with another woman, but even if he was, he always supported us." A man's financial loyalty to his family can trump all other forms of fidelity.

While women accept extended periods apart from male partners as necessary for the financial support of family, these separations—ostensibly temporary—often result in a permanent end to relationships. Final abandonment, then, is perhaps the most acute symptom of transnational gender imbalances, an infidelity that women individually and collectively fear. Repeatedly I heard the stories of women who have endured these ultimate betrayals, such as Paula, whose husband went to California, met a woman, and never again had contact with his wife and children. Or Raquel, who was pregnant when her husband left; she never heard from him, and it was a cousin who had to tell her, nearly a year after her husband's departure, of his other wife and newborn baby. Inevitably, women abandoned by their husbands must migrate, a difficult prospect in a community where male migration is the norm and female migration is discouraged or heavily orchestrated by male actors.

Men, too, operate within and outside of state power, but because of males' position within families, they are able to strategically use the power of the U.S. state to extend and fortify their existing control within families. This is an example of how state power works in tandem with migrants' understandings of gender. Numerous men who make the trip to "*el otro lado*" begin extramarital unions or abandon their families in Mexico, utilizing the U.S.-Mexico border as a barrier when it suits them. For example, Ernesto migrated to Albuquerque while his wife, Isadora, stayed in San Marcos with their four children. Within just a few months, Isadora heard through cousins that Ernesto was in a relationship with a woman. Ernesto rarely sent money, which was putting obvious strain on Isadora's household. I visited Isadora frequently in her home, and the impact of Ernesto's actions was evident. Isadora was constantly working—while other women could at least take a minute to sit and talk, Isadora was always running around, feeding the animals or on her way to the *milpas*. Isadora told me that her husband's infidelity was a source of deep shame for her and the children. Isadora called and pleaded with Ernesto to stop betraying his family, but he seemed unaffected by Isadora's distress.

Isadora's friends were understandably concerned and quite critical of Ernesto. "How can he treat his family this way?" asked one neighbor. "He should know better!" said one of the more outspoken women in the rancho. Women in the community helped out by lending Isadora money or preparing meals for the family. Although Isadora was uncomfortable accepting such gestures, she needed their help and appreciated their friendship. Ernesto and Isadora both realized that Isadora was in a profoundly disadvantaged position vis-à-vis Ernesto and vis-à-vis the U.S. state. In this case, Ernesto demonstrated flexibility within a transnational space and in his partnership even as he precariously built a life in the United States; Isadora, with extremely limited power within the family, was clearly constrained by state control. Loyalties and disloyalties surface precisely because of the broader sociopolitical context within which men and women are migrating or not.

Examining gender and kin relationships against the backdrop of state power and U.S. state-ascribed immigration status underscores how transnational Mexicans simultaneously experience limited flexibility and intense constraints as they migrate between Mexico and the United States. Despite—and paradoxically, sometimes because of or by harnessing—state controls, Mexican (im)migrants utilize strategies to reunite family, secure legal status in the United States, find fulfilling relationships, escape dissatisfying or dangerous unions, ensure financial or emotional support, and/or protect oneself and one's children from violence and abuse. Operating both within and outside of state controls—but always within a framework of emic and etic gendered politics—transnational migrants may marry a U.S. citizen, migrate to either country specifically to flee from or reunite with a partner, contact local law enforcement in the United States to have a spouse deported, or leave Mexico or the United States with their partner's child(ren). Family and gender ties are both severed and reunited within this complex web of state power characterized by control that is partial yet profound.

A Gendered Bind

Constructions of gender, on the part of migrants and within state regimes, create borderlands, shape gendered migrations, guide border crossings, and define the transgressions of intimate transnational relations. José's experience of crossing the border reveals the broad insecurity that comes with undocumented border crossings as well as the specifically gendered risks. The rape José witnessed is a powerful example of the gendered dimensions of U.S. immigration policy and the state's construction of illegality. This tragic event, which unfortunately is not an isolated case, again illustrates how migrations are gendered: the woman was the only female among a group of nearly twenty men. It also points to the ways that gender directs actual border crossings. In this case, fears about gendered violence at the border were realized; in fact, the risk of rape is often mentioned as the primary reason for not having women cross without documents. It is potential and actualized violence, as well as expectations of gendered behavior, that guides who stays and who goes, the divergent ways that men and women typically enter the United States without papers, and, by extension, gender relations in migrant communities. While the rape of this young woman may seem distant from actions of the U.S. government, state presence—with U.S. helicopters circling overhead and spotlights shining down—defined the space where the rape occurred. As the state carried out actions aimed at ostensibly protecting the nation, an individual especially vulnerable vis-à-vis the U.S. state, a young woman without documents, found herself in great danger.

Border crossings, position and power within relationships, one's options negotiating infidelity, intimate violence, and movement itself are gendered. Gendered borderlands have implications related to the security and insecurity of migrant families, how gendered relationships are structured and enacted, and the geographic locations of migrants depending on multiple aspects of the self. State power and the categorization of (im)migrants within the United States interact with migrants' constructions of gender relations and expectations of masculinity and femininity. Women and men move (or do not move) throughout the borderlands according to their gender positions. Women are repeatedly subject to control from the state and from the men in their lives. Men—agents with a relatively broad range of autonomy within the "gender hegemonies" (Ortner 1996: 18) that shape transnational lives—are nonetheless constrained by the intersections of masculinity, (il)legality, class, and race within the United States.

Both Benito and Delia, for example, are limited by the gendered aspects of migration. Several months after Benito had gone to the United States, I saw him in Albuquerque, at the home of his uncle, where he was living until he could afford an apartment of his own. His enthusiasm had notably waned. It was late in the evening when he arrived. He walked through the door, greeted me, and collapsed on the sofa. "I'm exhausted," he sighed. "I work all the time . . . I miss San Marcos. Tell me the news from the rancho." And when I most recently saw Delia in Mexico, little had changed in her day-to-day life: she continued to live with her parents and, despite her strong will and pleadings, she had not gone to the United States. Tellingly, she now strategized ways to migrate with the help of a man. "Maybe I'll marry someone who will take me there," she whispered after her mother left the room. "I still have hope that I will migrate someday." Lidia and her daughters did cross "*por la línea*" and made it safely across the border, although Lidia now spends most of the day alone in the family's apartment, isolated from the strong networks of women that she was part of in Mexico. And, José did not return to the United States; he does not know what happened to the woman who crossed with him that night. He did tell me, though, that he will never permit his daughters, now teenagers, to cross the border without documents.

Such findings underscore the risks and uncertainties of migrating without documents, for both women and men, and reveal the gendered character of power relations between partners and within families. My analysis points to the specifically gendered production of illegality. Gendered crossings and intimate relationships, often conceptualized as intimate spheres, are embedded, and arguably created, within a context that extends far beyond interpersonal exchanges between women and men. As David, who returned to the rancho after six years in the United States, told me: "You [Americans] want us, and at the same time, you don't want us." "Desire" in the United States for Mexican labor—and particularly male labor—directly translates into transnational relationships and gendered transgressions, underscoring the anthropologist Elizabeth Povinelli's assertion that "love is a political event" (Povinelli 2006: 175). Multiple desires—on the part of actors in both Mexico and the United States—do indeed "(re)produce and (re)inscribe" (Constable 2003: 144) transnational inequalities. Gendered borderlands are shaped by the construction of immigration status within the United States. Transnational gendered exchanges reflect broader socioeconomic realities, injustice that reaches beyond the gendered actions and interactions of everyday life, even as it is viscerally felt within them.

PART III

Children on the Move

6

Por Mis Hijos/For My Children

Early one morning, in Ciudad Juárez, on the U.S.-Mexico border, three young Mexican children—three, five, and six years old—waited with their grandmother in a relative's home on the outskirts of the city. They had been apart from their mother, Susana, for more than two years, and had not seen or heard from their father since he had migrated to Los Angeles three years earlier. Susana described to me years later that she had migrated north *"por mis hijos"*—meaning both *"for* my children" and *"because* of my children"—out of necessity to support her family, a common experience for women abandoned by their partners. When Susana first went to the United States, the children stayed in the rancho with their maternal grandmother. As the children waited that morning for the *coyota* who would facilitate their border crossing, moods shifted from melancholic to anxious. Meanwhile, Susana sat by the phone in Albuquerque, frightened at the thought of her children crossing without her, and yet no longer able to tolerate years of separation. The children had become accustomed to living in the rancho with their grandmother and extended family. Leaving Mexico, and their *abuelita*, to migrate to New Mexico was not easy for these young migrants or their grandmother, and the oldest child, Tía, who is now eighteen and a U.S. citizen, still remembers and recounts the pain of that life-altering morning. As the children sobbed and reached out to their grandmother, they were taken by the *coyota* to begin the eight-hour trip to be reunited with their mother.

The border crossing of Tía and her siblings—a story I have heard several times, from the perspective of the children, their mother, and their grandmother—points to several arguments related to migrant agency, age, and generation developed in this chapter.[1] As discussed, migrations cannot be separated from the intimate relations that shape and structure transnational movement. A focus on the youngest members of Mexican migrant communities and their experiences as they migrate or not reveals the ways that generation and age structure migration. Young people directly and indirectly guide migration, and migration processes are always mediated if not constituted by age/generation. This part of the book emphasizes how age intersects with family relations within global flows. Indeed, the migration of young people cannot be separated from the experiences of adults as they parent and care for children transnationally. Furthermore, the overlapping spheres of age and gender reveal expressions of—and restrictions on the—agency of young people. A focus on transnational children and youth problematizes categorization of one's agency and generation, even as such analysis demonstrates the utility of theorizing similarities and distinctions according to different aspects of subjectivity and experience.

My analysis of young people draws on two primary debates within anthropology and interdisciplinary migration studies. The first centers on immigrant "generation" and categorization by scholars that attempts to explain or understand the migration experience through one's place in stages of migration trajectories. This work identifies the commonalties, for example, among first- or second-generation immigrants, and how migrant experiences differ by generation, according to the timing of one's migration to a new place. The second related discussion focuses on agency, considering the extent to which young people act or not, within global flows. Young people of all ages—babies, toddlers, school children, teenagers, and young adults—are primary transnational actors, yet their agency is circumscribed by others according to age, gender, and generation.

The manner through which age is constructed and perceived is shifting ground: age and agency are relational or contextual, as is one's identification by self and others to a collective "generation." While fluidity characterizes multiple subjectivities, including gender, race/ethnicity, class, and sexuality, an understanding of age requires an especially flexible frame, in that the very character of age, however it may be constructed in diverse cultural contexts, is defined by change and movement through the life cycle (see Boehm et al. 2011). While there are arguably certain characteristics of the self that are more or less durable over one's lifetime, all individuals and groups experience and interpret changes related to age. As young people migrate (or not), movement—transnationally and through the life cycle—is constituted through and brings about change and even transformation.

The Transnational Generation:
Children Who Stay and Children Who Go

Despite an emphasis on adult migrants in much of the literature within migration studies, children are, in fact, prominent actors in migration flows. Children are both on the move and staying put, each significant processes for understanding transnational connections and disruptions. Transnationality results in a range of experiences that shape children's lives, as well as new kinship configurations and ways of caring for children. Within this transnational community, children and youth reside in, and migrate to and from, both Mexico and the United States. Migrant children move transnationally in diverse ways—by themselves, with one another, with their parents, under the care of extended family or community members, or with a *coyote* or a *coyota*—or young people may stay or be "left behind" in Mexico or the United States while their parents move, typically under the care of family members, including grandparents, aunts and uncles, or godparents.

In many ways, transnational Mexican children are "brought up across borders" (Levitt 2001: 75; see also Thorne et al. 2003), even when they have never migrated. Young people may be documented or undocumented migrants: they may be U.S. citizens or residents, or they may not have papers authorizing their migration to the United States. Their migrations can be from south to north, north to south, or circular. An infant crossing the border with false documents and the services of a *coyota*, an adolescent U.S. citizen who migrates to Mexico for the first time to join a deported parent, the child of migrants who has never been to the United States, or two siblings attending the same elementary school in the United States, one as a U.S. citizen and the other as an "illegal alien," capture a sampling of the varied circumstances of transnational children. The experiences of transnational children, then, include migrating or not migrating, and can involve young people with different configurations of national membership or U.S. immigration statuses.

Such diverse transnational experiences among children and youth challenge simplistic categorization of immigrant "generations." Much work in the social sciences—primarily by sociologists—utilizes categories of first- or second-generation immigrants, focuses on the particulars of U.S. immigration, and defines the second generation as children living in the United States (e.g., Kasinitz, Mollenkopf, and Waters 2004; Levitt and Waters 2002; Portes and Rumbaut 2001; Rumbaut and Portes 2001; see discussion in Boehm et al. 2011). While a generational framework in social scientific literature addressing migration has utility, it also has limitations. In large part, the delineation of generations as static categories stems from the study of "assimilation," a concept that is problematized through ethnographic research among children and families (see Boehm et al. 2011).

The categories of immigrant generations themselves demonstrate some of the challenges within such a typology: for example, as scholars have found diversity within first and second generations, new categories, including the

"1.5 generation" (see Rumbaut 2004) and ".5 generation" (see Brown 2009), have been developed. The first generation denotes those who migrate, and the second generation are children born to (im)migrant parents. The 1.5 generation, then, signifies children born in one country who migrate to another as children—and are therefore between the first and second generations—while the .5 generation includes elderly (im)migrants who presumably maintain ties to their home country more so than those who migrate as younger adults, and thus are not quite members of the first generation. These attempts to quantify generational membership illustrate both the multiple experiences of people according to age and place in the life cycle, and the persistence of labels within academic endeavor.

Generational categories do not fully capture the diversity of experiences or the contextual, shifting character of migration trajectories along lines of age and generation, and ethnographic research can provide insights about how age and generational relationships are perceived and made meaningful for transnational Mexicans. There are very divergent experiences of, for example, a six-month-old infant migrating to reunite with family, a fourteen-year-old labor migrant perceived as a man by his community, and a seventy-year-old woman crossing to meet her grandchildren for the first time. These "first-generation" migrants share little in their migration trajectories, and, especially in the case of the young man, can challenge culture-specific notions of youth and adulthood. While the infant migrant could be understood as part of the 1.5 generation and the elderly woman perceived as belonging to the .5 generation, the typologies do not easily capture diverse experiences and raise questions about where lines should be drawn within such categorization. The teenager is even more difficult to place, since he could be labeled as "1.5 generation"—since he first went to the United States before turning eighteen or as part of the "first generation" because he is perceived as an adult within the community. While it is useful to theorize different experiences, including along lines of generation and through constructions within the life cycle, an appropriate starting point considers the ways that migrants themselves understand, construct, and experience such groupings and divisions.

The work of Glick Schiller and Fouron about the "transnational second generation"—children born in "the homeland and the new land" (Glick Schiller and Fouron 2001: 175; see also Fouron and Glick Schiller 2002)—provides one way to complicate bounded categories or generations. Building on this framework, though without conceptualizing generations as numerically delineated categories, the next generation of Mexican (im)migrants can be conceptualized as it is understood among migrants themselves: children and youth living in both countries for whom labels of first and second generation are often not appropriate. This is a *"generación transnacional*/transnational generation" (Boehm 2008a: 784), in that they share diverse connections to transnationality. Although residents of San Marcos and neighboring communities have a long history of transnational movement between Mexico and the United States, individuals have often commented that today's children, youth, and young adults are experiencing transnationalism in unprecedented ways (see also Hess 2009; Smith 2006). Thus, "generation" can perhaps be more accurately conceived of as a spectrum of different life experiences among transnational children and youth. Such a continuum can include, for example, individuals who are born in either Mexico or the United States and who migrate north or south as children or young adults, children living in Mexico whose parents live and work in the United States most of the year, and children who divide their time between both countries.

When considering agency among young people, a continuum again serves as a way to conceptualize the possibilities for and limitations to acting within a transnational space. As "the ability to exert one's will and to act in the world" (Boehm et al. 2011: 7), agency is experienced on different levels and understood variably across cultural contexts. In public and even academic discourses, (im)migrants are typically characterized as adults. Such representations dismiss children and youth as actors at the center of migration processes, which they indisputably are. An analysis of agency among young people must also consider children and youth within webs of family and state regimes (Ong 1999), constrained by other actors ranging from parents and caregivers to state agents, and enacted along lines of age and gender. This is again "embedded agency" (Ortner 1996: 13) that is shaped by a range of structures.

Thus, young people of all ages are central actors within migration processes and display agency, although a continuum of autonomy finds infants at one end of the scale and young men at the other. From infants to adolescent boys who are viewed as men, children are actors who demonstrate agency and exercise more or less power according to aspects of the self, underscoring the importance of theorizing young people who go and stay, and the individuals with whom they interact. While the migration of young males from Mexico has a long history, it is increasingly common for very young children to migrate, including infants and toddlers. Gender, too, plays a role, and the age and gender of a child intersect to determine if/how a young migrant will cross. So, while it is common for male adolescents and teenagers to migrate independently, the migration of young children (both male and female) and of female adolescents is strictly controlled.

Still, while it is problematic to dismiss children as agents, children are not solely autonomous subjects. As with other aspects of transnational migration, the actions of children are always embedded in family relations and gendered politics. Agency is expressed according to age and family relations, demonstrating how the actions of children and youth—and the actions of adults—guide or control the movement and locations of young people transnationally. Similarly, understandings of masculinity and femininity facilitate and restrain the migrations of children and youth, playing a prominent role in determining their locations or placements throughout the transnation. Although children and youth are without question actors in migration processes, "agency" is always mediated by aspects of the self and relationships with others. Agency cannot thus be accurately characterized as that which young transnational Mexicans have or do not have: both the force of and limitations to agency can be seen by considering actions according to age.

(Dis)placing Children and Parents

"I feel it's best for my children to stay here with my mother," explained Nina as she offered me a cold orange soda. "It is so dangerous for them in the north . . . imagine if *la migra* were to find us!" Nina's children, Isabel, age seven, and Beto, age four, have migrated north and south repeatedly in their short lifetimes. Although Nina is concerned about their safety in the United States, her unease is primary because of her own undocumented status: the children are both U.S. citizens, born in Texas while their parents were working there. When the children's father left Nina for another woman, she returned with Isabel and Beto to San Marcos for a brief period. The children then lived in San Marcos with their maternal grandparents for nearly two years while Nina worked in the United States. Nina went first to San Diego, where she worked in temporary positions cleaning office buildings. Eventually, she moved to Arkansas to be with her new partner from a neighboring rancho, Humberto.

When Nina became pregnant, she decided it was again time to reunite her family. Her young children traveled by car—a two-day trip—with Humberto's brother to the United States. Nina told me that she had reservations about having her children travel alone with her partner's brother and two other men she did not know well but felt it was the safest, or the least dangerous, way to reunite with her children. When I visited with Nina one summer, she and the children had just returned to Mexico with plans for Isabel and Beto to begin another extended stay in the rancho, but when I spoke with

Nina later by phone, she told me that the children were again with her in the United States. Still, Nina lamented, she often considers having the children return to San Marcos because of the sense of security she has when her children are in Mexico.

As with the migration of Tía and her siblings, the transnational movement of Isabel and Beto demonstrates several points. First, these children are transnational actors who have migrated repeatedly, beginning as toddlers, between Mexico and the United States. Their experiences challenge notions of Mexican migrants as solely adult agents within labor flows. Because of their young age, their migrations are perhaps more accurately understood as "placements," orchestrated and facilitated by parents and other adult caregivers, an experience that is quite different from that of adolescent boys who display notable autonomy as they migrate. The "circulation of children," then, must be considered within the broader political-economic context and the decisions parents make to ensure their children's well-being (Leinaweaver 2008). The (dis)placements and migrations of young people are inevitably linked to parents' migrations and the experience of caring for children transnationally.

Children are actors, and yet children's actions are almost always mediated by adults: parents, grandparents, aunts and uncles, as well as those involved in the industry of border crossing. This is especially clear in cases of very young children, infants, and toddlers whose migrations are entirely orchestrated by adults. The migration of Susana's children, for example, took place after months of planning and arrangements made by adult actors. Susana, in consultation with her siblings and friends, located a *coyota* trusted by others—a woman with children of her own—and when it was time for the children to cross, the children's grandmother brought them to stay with extended family and arranged to meet the *coyota*. While the *coyota* was well recommended, there are obvious risks inherent to such border crossings. According to the grandmother, meeting the *coyota* and physically putting the children in her care was especially important. She told me that she was not going to trust someone with her grandchildren until she met her in person and looked her in the eye. Understandably, the migration of very young children is carefully arranged by parents and other family members.

Adults, then, have significant power in the lives of their children, and they do not always agree with one another about how migrations should be carried out. For example, Mercedes explained to me that when her daughter, Frida, was just five years old, her brother-in-law and his wife suggested that Frida go to the United States to attend school. "They said that the schools were very good, and that Frida would be so fortunate to go to classes there. So I agreed to let them take her to Dallas." Mercedes said that Frida's aunt and uncle had been unable to have children, and that they wanted to adopt Frida and raise her as their own daughter. They assured Mercedes that, of course, Frida would visit often, but Mercedes told me that as their departure date neared, the bad feeling she had about the situation intensified. The morning that they were scheduled to leave, Mercedes would not permit Frida to go. While it did cause a rift in the family for some time, Mercedes was never sorry about the decision she made. In the case of Frida, several adults negotiated her placement in a transnational space.

This seeming contradiction, then, of children as actors and children as those whose actions are orchestrated by others, is central to all migrations—the movement and placement of adults and young people—pointing to the utility of an analysis that connects the shifting fields of agency of children and their parents. Migrations can be traced within family and kin relations. When parents "place" young people in diverse locales, they are acting for their families and fulfilling their responsibilities as parents and caregivers. Throughout my fieldwork, transnational Mexicans have indicated that a primary motivation for migrating is their children (see also Constable 2004; Dreby 2010; Orellana et al. 2001; Parreñas 2005; Pribilsky 2007). Although migrants have slightly different perspectives on this theme—nearly everyone describes the need to financially support family, some hope for a different life for their children than they have in Mexico, while others identify educational opportunities in the United States—the words "for my children" have become a kind of trope linking migration to the next generation. As one mother described, "There are advantages for me, but above all, I migrate for my children . . . I have to think about them, so that they can have a better life." Even as the actions of young people are directed by adult actors, children and youth are at the center of migration processes.

Family is understood first and foremost as a means of financial support, especially for children. Kin ties are the primary structure through which children are provided for—above all economically, though also emotionally, socially, and educationally. For the majority of migrants, the decision to go to the United States is tightly bound to cultural understandings of parenthood and its obligations: Mexicans migrate specifically to fulfill their role as parents and providers. As discussed, the expectations of parents and need for adults to migrate are markedly gendered. When men migrate they embody masculinity and realize their responsibility to provide financially for family (as a comparison, see Parreñas 2005). For mothers, the motivations to migrate are especially complicated—women typically migrate to reunite with a male partner or because of the necessity to work after being abandoned by a spouse (see chap. 5). Transnational parenthood, and particularly "transnational" (Hondagneu-Sotelo and Avila 1997) or "transborder" (Stephen 2007) motherhood, is indeed riddled with difficult decisions, ambivalent emotions, and multiple negotiations in the face of limited options.

Both men and women express the sentiment that their children are the primary motivation for migration. Single mothers have very few options, and the need to provide for children nearly always drives a woman's "independent" migration. Men, too, understand their migrations as linked to the need to provide for family, especially their children. One father, Tito, explained during a family visit in the rancho before again leaving for the north: "Why do I migrate? I migrate for my children." Although Tito has U.S. permanent residency and could petition for his wife and children, he told me that he has decided that his family should remain in Mexico. "I do not want my children living in the United States," he said. "I migrate for them, to benefit them." Here, migration takes place at the intersection of family ties and family position. Family relations are significant, and responsibility to kin—especially children—is strong.

At the same time, family is, simply stated, the people you (ideally) live with: for migrants it is a priority to reside in close proximity to family members. With the transforming familial relations ushered in through migration, though, family residence rarely actualizes this ideal (see chap. 2). Thus, parents aim to secure care for children through their residence with, in order of preference, both parents, the mother, or extended female kin, typically the maternal grandmother or a maternal aunt. This is a significant shift from earlier patrilocal kinship formations, one that is transforming the character of parenting. Given this shifting ground of residence transnationally, securing children's cohabitation with parents, mothers, and/or female kin takes on increased significance.

It is at the intersection of these two priorities among Mexican families— economic support and the co-residency of children and (especially female) caregivers—that this transnational predicament emerges: providing economically for children and partners means that parents and children cannot always reside in the same nation-state. Financially supporting family and physically being with family cannot be actualized solely in Mexico, and so transmigrants are continuously negotiating multiple locations where kin may reside in tandem with diverse and shifting configurations of family. Decisions about how and where to situate parents and children are complicated, ongoing, and inevitably anxiety-producing, creating what one mother described as "a pain in my heart." There is a complex web of motivations that parents consider, including economics, basic needs of food and housing, work opportunities, and/or aspirations to improve the lives of their children. There are diverse circumstances in which families find themselves along with a range of choices parents must make given the ever-changing conditions they navigate—sometimes migrating and other times not, choosing to migrate without children, reuniting family in the United States, and/or having children move north or south for temporary or extended periods. The choices that parents make are difficult ones, based on the shifting circumstances of a given moment.

It may seem curious to include the experiences of adults in an analysis of children—and indeed the literature on parenting across borders has been criticized for not sufficiently focusing on the perspectives of young people—but there is a need to consider the agency and experiences of migrants across generations as necessarily intertwined. Just as parents and their migrations cannot be disconnected from their children, the actions of young people must be considered as embedded within relationships with adult caregivers. This is, in fact, "child-centered research," especially given that the migrations of adults within this community are nearly always understood as centered on children. An understanding of children's agency includes the recognition of parents as agents in children's lives, albeit to varying degrees, depending on family position, age, and gendered politics.

Gender Rites

Tadeo has proven himself to be strong man. When he was a teenager, Tadeo went north with a group of other young men from the rancho. Their border crossing was harrowing—they attempted to cross many times before they were successful . . . by foot, in a train, with a *coyote*, swimming across the Rio Grande. Eventually they made it to the other side, where Tadeo spent three years busing tables and saving money. At twenty-one, he was back in San Marcos. His longtime girlfriend, Erica, waited for him while he was in the United States, and soon after he returned they were married. When I visited with them, they were expecting a baby and thinking about the next trip north. Tadeo told me he would probably go alone, and that Erica and the baby would stay with his parents. He said his mother had counseled him that it would be best for Erica to stay behind—he was, after all, the man of the family. He had a responsibility to migrate, to work and earn money in order to build a house and support his wife and baby.

The previous section focused on the situations in which the agency of parents trumps that of children; this section turns to adolescents as they transition to adulthood to further consider how young people both act and are constrained within different contexts. Age is not the only axis along which to explore agency among children: autonomy among transnational youth is also, and always, enabled and limited by constructions of gender (see also Smith 2006). The rites of passage through which youth become adults—for males, migrating to the United States, and for females, their *quinceañera* or fifteenth birthday celebration—are processes through which age and gender intersect. If infants who migrate by their parents' design represent one pole of experience, young men represent the other. Comparing young women and men illustrates that age alone is not adequate for understanding expressions of agency through the life cycle. While adolescent boys can be perceived of as adults early in the teen years—and granted the freedom to move transnationally and exercise autonomy in their lives—as girls age, they continue to be treated as young children. While autonomy increases with age, such agency is inevitably mediated by gender.

Tadeo's experience is typical of young men from rural communities in this region of Mexico. They are permitted—indeed, often expected—to go to the United States when they are very young, at the age of fifteen, sixteen, or seventeen, and sometimes as young as twelve or thirteen. For males of the next generation who were born in the United States or who migrated as children, migration is already an integral part of their personhood, and for adolescent males living in Mexico, they are expected to go north. Migration is a principal ritual through which boys become men—"a patriarchal rite of passage" (Hondagneu-Sotelo 1994: 83)—linking migration to the life cycle (see also Hawkins et al. 2010; Pribilsky 2007; Smith 2006). While migration is a primary rite of passage through which boys become men and enact masculinity, adolescent females are actively discouraged from migrating. Girls become women by way of another path, following quite a different trajectory as they come of age.

It is common for young men to experience this ritual together—crossing as a group and then living in an apartment with other young men, and working at the same restaurant or business as friends from their home community. I spoke with sixteen-year-old Paco a few weeks before he left for New Mexico. I ran into Paco at one of the rancho's *tiendas*—he was with friends, playing a video game that the storeowner had recently purchased. Paco explained that he would be accompanied by two other teens from San Marcos, a cousin and a friend. The group would first travel to Ciudad Juárez, where Paco's brother had arranged for the boys to meet a trustworthy *coyote*. Since the *coyote* had been hired by other residents of the rancho, Paco's brother felt secure with the arrangement. The *coyote* would lead the boys by foot across the border to a predetermined site in El Paso where another cousin would be waiting to drive Paco and the group to Albuquerque. Paco said that there would be plenty of work for the teens once they arrived—he explained that his brother worked for a concrete company and his cousins bused tables at a large restaurant, so Paco was confident that between the two businesses he would quickly find employment.

When boys who have migrated return to Mexico after working in the United States, they are then viewed by community members as men. Like Tadeo, after coming back to the rancho, young men typically marry, start a family, and begin to work their own parcel of land, before again migrating to the United States. Another young man, Estefan, came back to San Marcos after two and a half years in Dallas. Estefan, who was nineteen years old when he returned, was welcomed by his family and members of the community. Estefan quickly started attending dances, and within a few months, met a young woman from a nearby rancho. A brother living in Albuquerque offered his vacant home to Estefan and his *novia*. Soon after the couple moved in and set up their home, Estefan began planning for his next trip north. He told me that he would not stay in San Marcos for long—while he was glad that he had been able to help with the family farm for a period of time, he needed to return to Texas and work. Similarly, young men who have grown up in the United States will travel to Mexico, if they are able to do so, to meet and date young women, and ideally find a partner.

In striking contrast, consider another teen, Mayra. As Mayra and I spoke, she was working on a needlepoint project, sewing a red rose in the center of a small linen that would keep tortillas warm. "I'm very bored here in the rancho," she told me. "There is nothing to do!" Mayra wanted to go to high school—she was one of the most accomplished students in the middle school, and her teachers encouraged her to continue her studies, but because the only high school was an hour away, her family could not afford the cost of transportation and meals. Mayra's family did put money together, however, to have a *quinceañera* when she turned fifteen. Her father and brothers saved up wages from their work in the United States to help fund the celebration. Since the important ritual had taken place a few years earlier, Mayra has been able to attend the *bailes* and socialize with young men, but she told me that she doesn't want to get married anytime soon. Mayra is already a housewife—her mother has health problems and, as the eldest daughter living at home, domestic chores are her responsibility. Her two older brothers went to the other side without documents when they were teenagers and have not returned to the rancho for many years. Mayra said she would like to visit her brothers in the United States, but her parents will not permit her to go without the required paperwork. The family made a trip to the U.S. consulate in Monterrey, but their applications for tourist visas were denied. They may try again next year, but in the meantime Mayra is resigned to stay in San Marcos. She has joined a soccer team, and, she tells me, she has plenty of time to complete various needlepoint projects.

As Mayra's experience demonstrates, the path for girls to womanhood is quite different from that through which boys transition to manhood. Boys become men through migration to the United States, but females' passage to adulthood is often characterized by staying in one place. Young women are likely to have a *quinceañera* celebration, and then essentially pass time doing domestic chores in their family's home until marriage, when they move in with their husband and are responsible for domestic tasks within a new household. The *quinceañera* is an important ritual in the lives of young women (see also Napolitano 2002). This religious ceremony and fiesta marks the transformation through which a girl becomes a woman. In addition, the *quinceañera* is significant for everyone around the fifteen-year-old: it is a time when family members pool resources and travel north or south to join the event. The celebration is a source of great pride for parents, grandparents, extended family members, and the community. These events take place in both Mexico and the United States, and individual families determine the location of the *quinceañera* based on different factors including the legal status and location of family members as well as resources for bands and venues available in each locale.

A *quinceañera* I attended in Albuquerque further demonstrates how age and gender intersect in the lives of young people. On the morning of the event, the young woman turning fifteen, Elisa, was looking into her mother's dresser mirror—framed by hand-crocheted doilies and several rosaries—as her cousins pulled her hair in opposite directions. They were forming perfectly polished ringlets, placing them on top of Elisa's head. Elisa was born in Mexico but has lived in Albuquerque for the past decade, arriving when she was just beginning elementary school. Her *quinceañera* was a transnational event—although it was held in Albuquerque, family members on both sides of the border had participated in its preparations. As her cousins shook a can of hair spray and took aim, I asked Elisa why the *quinceañera* was an important event for her. She shrugged, "I'm just happy that I will be able to go out alone with my friends . . . with boys. Honestly, I think my mom is more excited about it than I am!" And Elisa's mother certainly had been looking forward to this celebration. For more than a year, she had spent much of her free time planning for the event; she was thrilled and a bit relieved that the big day had finally arrived.

After a mass held at the family's parish, there was a dinner and dance at an event center. The tables were covered with white tablecloths, dinner was served on fine china, and a popular band from Texas had traveled to New Mexico for the event. One of the night's highlights was a ritual that marked Elisa's passage to womanhood: after dinner, Elisa sat on a chair in the middle of the dance floor, and her father bent down and put high heels on his daughter, presumably for the first time. Afterwards, Elisa explained to me that this ritual is part of every *quinceañera* she has attended, and signifies the point when the young woman can begin dancing with men. Elisa's first dance was with her father—father and daughter shared the dance floor for a moment and then it quickly filled with couples.

As Elisa's family prepared for the *quinceañera*, her grandmother told me how special this ritual is for everyone: "It is when the *paloma* [dove] flies," she said. "It is something very beautiful." However, this image—of the young woman as a dove set free—sharply contrasts with the reality for most young women, in both Mexico and the United States. In actuality, after females celebrate their fifteenth birthday, they pass most of their time working in their family's home until they marry, still subjected to what can be intense parental control. For example, shortly after her *quinceañera*, Elisa, who had looked forward to the independence she would gain, described how controlling her mother continued to be: "She never wants me to go out. She doesn't approve of my friends . . . and my boyfriend—she won't even acknowledge him! He has never been inside our house. My parents act like he doesn't exist." Similarly, Dina, a young woman living in the rancho, told me that her parents would often prevent her from attending the *bailes* after her *quinceañera*, and when she started dating a young man from a neighboring town, he was not permitted to visit Dina at home. I asked Dina when her parents would be likely to meet her boyfriend of eighteen months, and she replied: "Who knows?" Dina's mother said it was unlikely that they would interact with the young man unless a wedding took place.

In contrast to boys and men, girls and young women are especially controlled in cases of migration (see chap. 5). An example is when a young woman, Jimena, traveled with her uncles to Dallas to attend school when she was thirteen. She has now graduated from high school and is taking classes at a community college, but because she is undocumented, she has not been able to return and see her parents and siblings since she left six years ago. Her mother, Linda, often talked with me about having a daughter so far from home. Linda recounted the day that Jimena left—what she described as the saddest day of her life. It was clear that she had felt pressured by her husband and her brothers-in-law to send Jimena to the United States so that she would have educational opportunities. Linda said that, while she was very proud of Jimena's accomplishments, she also regretted that she had permitted her to go. "I think of my daughter every day," Linda told me. "No parent should have to be separated from a child like that."

These are gendered politics that move transnationally. The trajectories of young people do not always follow the same patterns, although there are surprising similarities. The independence that young men experience through migration extends to the United States, as do the restrictions placed on the "autonomy, mobility, and personal decision making" (Espiritu 2003b: 279) of young women (see also Ong 2003). Although parents control, or at least attempt to control, the movement of young women on both sides of the border, female teens in Mexico are especially restricted. Like Mayra, young women repeatedly told me about the boredom they experience in the rancho. Few youth in the rancho, but especially young females, are able to continue their studies at the area's high school, and so the daily activities of girls and young women typically center on domestic responsibilities; this is a process through which parents "discipline their daughters as racial/national subjects as well as gendered ones" (Espiritu 2003a: 173).

Families in Mexico are often ambivalent about having their sons go to the United States, but they rarely prevent them from doing so. For daughters, however, familial attitudes about migration are notably distinct, and young women simply do not have access to migration in the same way that men do. In conversations about women and migration, there is almost certainly a mention of the "*peligro* [danger]" that young women who migrate must face. Families do not want and essentially do not permit young, unmarried daughters to go to the other side. In the previous chapter, I described how Delia was prevented from migrating, while Benito's migration was valued, and how José was adamant that his daughters would never migrate on their own and without documents. This is the contested terrain of migration and transnationality among young women and men.

The transformation of boys into men takes place precisely through movement, while the rite of passage through which girls become women culminates in stasis and confinement in the home, first as a devoted daughter and later, as a good wife. Certainly gender roles do not neatly fit within a reified production-reproduction dichotomy—in fact, there are constant negotiations of power between and among males and females. For example, there are young women who defy their parents and go out on dates, who migrate without parental approval, or who exercise more subtle forms of resistance, such as slowly or inadequately completing household chores. And, there are young men who choose not to migrate. Still, the actions of these young people are exceptions to strong patterns in gendered behavior. The contexts within which exchanges take place are often restrictive, and there is significant social pressure for youth to behave in specifically gendered ways. While the space to "act" increases with age, it is mediated by and intersects with gender subjectivities and expectations.

Plotting Agency across Generations

While agency is expressed in diverse forms, one's age and generation, relation to family members, and gender are significant in shaping the spaces that enable or limit autonomy and the ability to act. The (dis)placement of children, especially very young children, by parents and other adult caregivers illustrates how the actions of young people as migrants are often determined by adults, with very young children exercising little or no autonomy within transnational movement. On the other end of the continuum, male teenagers—viewed as adults by community members—practice a great deal of independence through migration. As young people age, differences in gender become increasingly prominent, with parallels in the ways that young women and children are perceived, demonstrating how age and agency are mediated by gender.

Young people, then, are actors with a range of options and levels of independence and confinement based on gender, age, family relations, and immigration status, among other factors. The movement of children and youth is always mediated by positionality and relationships with others. These are indeed children on the move—even when they do not migrate—negotiating positionality and self, as well as relationships with others, as they move through the life cycle. The experiences of young people further draw out the complexities and interconnectedness of intimate lives and state power. Divergent immigration statuses and national membership play out in particular ways in the lives of young people. A focus on children and youth enhances our understandings of state power, as well as the inseparability of productive and reproductive spheres.

7

Here–Not Here

I spent an afternoon in Mexico with a friend, Liliana, as she cared for a cha-
otic house full of children. They ran back and forth between the living room
where we were talking and a dusty courtyard filled with goats and chickens.
"Come *niños*," she called to the two smallest of the group. "I have someone for you to meet." Liliana introduced me to her grandsons, Héctor and
Claudio, aged two and five. "They have been here for nearly a year," Liliana
explained. "My son and daughter-in-law—they are *mojados*, as you know—
and so it is safer for the boys to be here with me. Their parents work all the
time, so really it is better this way." Liliana went on to describe the difficulties
her daughter-in-law was having, being so far from her young children. "But,
the boys are U.S. citizens," Liliana proclaimed proudly. "They are the Americans in the family . . . aren't you, *mis cariños*?!" She teased her grandsons, as
they ran out of the room laughing. Héctor and Claudio are, in many ways
here and yet *not here*, U.S. citizens with a form of contingent citizenship—
they are citizens of the United States living in Mexico explicitly because of
the undocumented status of their parents.

While chapter 6 considered migrants' constructions of age/generation and
how they intersect with family position and gender, this chapter explores how
state power and (il)legality are laid over such understandings, and how categorization by the state plays out in the lives of young people.[1] The experiences
of young people underscore spatial and symbolic shifts in understandings of
national belonging and exclusion among individuals within undocumented
(im)migrant families or families of mixed U.S. legal status. Among Mexican
(im)migrant families, the legal status of individual family members vis-à-vis
the U.S. state has concrete implications for the well-being of both documented
and undocumented children. The construction of (il)legality creates unstable,
contingent national membership in particular ways among children and youth.

The lived experiences of any transnational Mexican cannot be neatly slotted into immigration status as defined by the U.S. state, although the youngest members of families move in and out of different forms of citizenship in

specific ways. As the lived experiences of children illustrate, such categories are always subject to leakage, despite confidence in the integrity of boundaries on the part of the state and its members. Through the construction of "aliens" and "citizens," the state creates shifting or contingent citizenship for children within transnational mixed-status families. As the historian Mae M. Ngai argues, "The line between legal and illegal status can be crossed in both directions" (Ngai 2004: 6). The physical movement and geographic and symbolic locations of children reveal the instability—including the flexibility (Ong 1999) and exclusionary aspects—of citizenship itself.

The Instability of Citizenship

Different layers of citizenship—including the state's denial to recognize national membership—exist for Mexicans in the United States: undocumented residents do not hold legally ascribed membership or citizenship, permanent residents maintain a limited kind of membership, and Mexicans who have naturalized as U.S. citizens are arguably excluded from "cultural citizenship" (Flores and Benmayor 1997; Maira 2009; Rosaldo 1997; Rosaldo and Flores 1997; Stephen 2003) because of ethnic prejudice and racism. Multiple forms of citizenship are also undermined because of gender inequalities (e.g., Goldring 2001; Yuval-Davis and Anthias 1989; Yuval-Davis and Werbner 1999). To some extent, Mexicans who are permanent residents of the United States live as partial citizens in this country because they do not have the same rights as U.S. citizens—including the right to vote—although they must fulfill some of the same responsibilities as U.S. citizens—such as registering with the Selective Service and paying taxes. Of course, Mexicans who live in the United States without documents are excluded from formal citizenship or membership: undocumented Mexican (im)migrants are denied legal U.S. citizenship as well as broader civil citizenship or cultural citizenship that guarantees basic human rights.

Citizenship includes rights and responsibilities: state-ascribed citizenship both denotes membership in a collective and outlines the relationship between an individual and the state (Jacobson 1996: 7). Historically specific notions of citizenship are increasing problematized in a transnational world. As people move about the globe and across the boundaries of nation-states, narrow legal definitions of national membership are called into question. Indeed, "while diaspora is inherently a mobile activity, citizenship is intrinsically defined as a sedentary one" (Laguerre 1998: 10). Whether migration reinforces the power of states (e.g., Aretxaga 2003) or is resulting in citizenship's "decline" (Jacobson 1996), citizenship as a construct that is definitively attached to one nation-state remains powerful in people's lives, even as its relevance in everyday lives is challenged.

An expanding notion of citizenship can include forms of national membership that emerge from real practices and human agency (Jonas 1996; Laguerre 1998), and can allow for shifting membership in "imagined communities" (Anderson 1991). Many perceive "nationality as a human right" and call on the state to be accountable to "all its *residents* on the basis of international human rights law" (Jacobson 1996: 10). Beyond the issues related to legal or state-ascribed citizenship, scholars have raised questions about whether or not people of color ever acquire full citizenship in the United States, regardless of their legal status (see for example, Flores 1997; Rosaldo 1997; Rosas 2007): "being a citizen guarantees neither full membership in society nor equal rights . . . even when Latinos are U.S.-born citizens, they have been treated as second-class or third-class citizens" (Flores 1997: 255). United States citizenship, both legal and symbolic, can be difficult and, in many cases impossible for Mexicans to obtain. This underscores the fact that many Mexicans, regardless of legal membership, continue to live in the United States without the benefits of multiple forms of citizenship.

Scholars have proposed alternative ways of conceptualizing citizenship in a transnational world. Some have suggested that "transnational citizenship" (Bauböck 1994; Besserer 1998) captures the ways that membership transcends nation-state structures as a "de-territorialized citizenship that is not bounded to the notion of nationality" (Besserer 1998: 2). Similarly, "diasporic citizenship" (Laguerre 1998) is membership that "decenters the previous juridico-political definition of citizenship and invokes the centrality of its social, civil and political components" (Laguerre 1998: 190). And, rather than implying membership in a global community, "universal citizenship" (Jacobson 1996: 10) accounts for the expanding relevance of an international framework. Regardless of different ways of defining or labeling such alternative forms of membership, transnational movement underscores the need to create a global framework in which all individuals are protected.

A discussion of (trans)national membership, then, considers human agency within the authority of reconfiguring state structures. While new concepts of citizenship are evolving through actual practices, the everyday lives of transnational Mexicans present a challenge to, and are restricted by, nation-state borders. By building families transnationally, participating as members of communities in both Mexico and the United States, and constructing lives that are rooted in two nations, individuals propose emergent nationalities and new definitions of citizenship. Still, many alternative concepts of belonging are not yet acknowledged by the state, and transnational residents continue to be legally excluded, subjected to narrow laws and practices related to membership. The state also undermines the citizenship of its "legal" members, creating a form of contingent citizenship that can be flexible yet constraining for transnational Mexicans.

Contingent citizenship is national membership that is partial, conditional, or relational: contingent citizens include U.S. citizens who are culturally, socially, politically, or physically excluded from the nation, as well as undocumented residents of the United States who are de facto members by virtue of their employment, education, residence, political participation, and civic engagement. Constructed as simultaneously *here* and *not here*, transnational Mexican children especially move through layers of belonging and exclusion, "en route" (Coutin 2005) to distinct physical places and the embodiment of particular state categories. Nearly all members of migrant communities, but especially children and youth, experience the effects of contingent citizenship, underscoring the generalized vulnerability of transnational subjects. Building on the literature that explores the shifting and often problematic character of "citizenship," my conceptualization of contingent citizenship stems from the experiences of transnational children and youth.

Spaces of Citizenship and Exclusion

Much of the research about illegality employs metaphors of space to analyze state actions. De Genova focuses on the character of "boundaries," those that are not only geographic but also racial, economic, political, and cultural: "The social condition of transnational migrants . . . must be understood as a preeminently spatialized one" (De Genova 2005: 95). For Coutin, the locations of unauthorized Salvadorans, "legal nonsubjects," are tellingly characterized as "spaces of nonexistence" (Coutin 2000: 27): "There are multiple nonexistences and gradations of existence. It might be most accurate to say that, like characters who experience a temporal rift in a Star Trek episode, [undocumented migrants] come in and out of existence and exist simultaneously in multiple ways" (Coutin 2000: 27). In the anthropologist Nathalie Peutz's work, Somali nationals deported from the United States are "out-laws," physically removed deportees who are also "cast outside of the law" (Peutz 2007: 189), while the sociologist Carolyn Pinedo Turnovsky describes how undocumented migrants claim a "place" of their own looking for work on a street corner (Turnovsky 2006: 61). Spatial understandings of inclusion and exclusion—the spaces "between" (Gutiérrez 1996; Hellman 2008; Jones-Correa 1998)—impact migrants, especially children and youth, in particular ways.

In the novel *The Pickup*, Nadine Gordimer similarly captures the spatial movement and exclusion of undocumented migrants. Describing an unauthorized migrant, Gordimer explores the shifting character of national membership: "He is here, and he is not here. It's within this condition of existence that they exist." (Gordimer 2002: 37). It is significant that he (Abdu) is "here" and "not here," and yet this is the condition within which they both—Abdu and his partner Julie, a citizen of South Africa—"exist" (Gordimer 2002). This underscores overlapping or intersecting territorial and intimate spaces. While individuals do have particular experiences based on their immigration status within the United States, they must be considered within gendered, familial relationships. Shifts in membership—this notion of contingent citizenship—stems from family relations and is differentially experienced according to one's gender and age.

As outlined, migrants are always members of families and communities. State action and exclusion are not focused only on the individual "illegal alien." It is instead a family affair: the state's production of illegality among particular family members creates a form of contingent citizenship for all members of undocumented and mixed-status families, including those who are legally recognized as citizens. The production of illegality—by definition focused on the individual—has profound implications for children and youth as they migrate and do not migrate. This is "alienation" (Coutin 2000) that results in the categorization of children as "alien" by association. In other words, the unauthorized status of individual family members is extended to others. The categorization of individual migrants as "aliens" who are "legal" or "illegal" impacts all members of transnational migrant networks, although such categories are applied to the youngest migrants in particular ways.

Migrant children and youth uniquely reveal contingent citizenship, this conditional and unstable relationship to the nation-state. Six-month-old Julia, who crossed with her mother and a *coyota* last month; Tonio, an undocumented migrant about to graduate with a degree in biochemistry; and Juan and Daniela, U.S. citizens living in Mexico while their mother works cleaning hotel rooms in Los Angeles—their lives must be understood in relation to the U.S. state and the many state actions that permeate intimate spheres. Women, men, and children of all ages are moving and staying in a transnational context. An analysis of "illegality," a construct that categorizes *individuals* as unauthorized migrants, demonstrates how its construction in fact targets groupings of people—families and communities—and young people within these networks.

The placements and displacements of children—as *here* and *not here*—are often attributed in public discourse to the "sins" of migrant parents. This reasoning asserts parents' responsibility and even culpability for putting children at risk. Individuals representing divergent positions within the debate about immigration—including those who support immigration reform and a form of amnesty as well as proponents of heavily restricted immigration or closed borders—find common ground in their focus on parents' agency, agreeing that parents are responsible for children's vulnerabilities. For example, a spokesperson for the Immigration and Customs Enforcement agency, Kelly Nantel, stated that "parents are putting their children in these difficult situations" (cited in Preston 2007) while journalist Justin Draeger questions if migrant children should be penalized for "the sins of their fathers [*sic*]" (Draeger 2007). The explanation for transnational children at risk: "children are impacted negatively by the decisions of their parents" (Nantel cited in Preston 2007).

Yet, as discussed, the decisions parents make about the spatial placements for themselves and their children cannot be easily cast as simply individual choices. Driven by necessity and tempered by their negotiations with state power (Hess and Shandy 2008: 265), parents make decisions within a cloud of insecurity and aware of the possible outcomes they and their children may experience. Parents, of course, recognize and weigh the multiple risks their children face: separation from parents, the dangers of crossing the border, or the perils of reuniting families with undocumented members in the United States, among others. Parents lament the insecure climate at the border and within the United States, describing their situation as an inevitable bind and choosing what they may perceive as the only option or the least uncertain trajectory among few alternatives. It is these dangers that lead parents to leave children, including U.S. citizens, in Mexico with extended family or to decide, typically after years of living apart, to bring children to the United States. The choices parents make and the risks they and/or their children manage, then, come out of an environment characterized by emic notions of family but also, notably, state practices.

This again points to the actions of adult caregivers in the lives of young people, illustrating that while parents certainly make decisions to (dis)place children transnationally (see chap. 6), there are questions related to the degree to which parents themselves exercise agency in borderland spaces. In large part, the spatial shifts of children stem from a dilemma in transnational lives: a primary motivation for migration is to support and benefit children, yet the (dis)placements—and the resulting contingent citizenship—of children in Mexico or the United States occur precisely because of migration. Given the context within which Mexican migrants of all ages navigate the U.S. state, the notion of choice is problematic, emphasizing the complicated backdrop against which parents and children migrate north and south within a transnational space.

Young people are moving between Mexico and the United States, with and without documents. The transnational movement of children as unauthorized migrants is part a of broader process that shapes migration to and from the United States: according to the Pew Hispanic Center, approximately one-sixth of the U.S. undocumented population, some 1.7 million people, is under eighteen years of age (Passel 2005). Such research provides a more accurate profile of those labeled "illegal aliens"; while public and political discourse would have us believe that undocumented migrants are adult men, undocumented migrants are increasingly very young children, including infants and toddlers (see also Silva et al. 2010). Additionally, as the number of undocumented migrants living in the United States increases, the number of U.S. citizen children with parents who are undocumented is growing. My analysis focuses on diverse groups: children living in the United States without papers, U.S. citizen children living in the United States with family members who are undocumented, children in Mexico without the documentation required to "legally" migrate, and U.S. citizen children living in Mexico with their parents or under the care of others.

Young people have divergent experiences because of different legal statuses, family relations, subject positions, and geographic locations, but they also share similar experiences, largely through interactions with and categorization by the U.S. state. How the state does (or does not) define individual migrant children in relation to the nation depends on the status of parents, siblings, and other family members and their place within families. Contingent citizenship among children and youth is a tenuous form of national membership that creates what Ngai defines as *alien citizens* (Ngai 2004: 2) as well as what I understand to be *citizen aliens*.

Alien Citizens: Here, Not Here

As I spoke with his mother, three-year-old Emilio peered at me from a doorway, disappearing for periods and then peeking out again. "Since we arrived a few weeks ago, he has been very tentative with people," explained Juanita. "Even his *tías* [aunts] seem to scare him!" When we spoke, Juanita and Emilio had recently arrived in the rancho following the deportation of Juanita's husband. Emilio, like Héctor and Claudio, is among a growing group of

U.S. citizen children who are currently living in Mexico. In the daily lives of transnational families, the state produces these *alien citizens*, U.S. citizens who, according to Ngai, "are presumed to be foreign by the mainstream of American culture and, at times, by the state (Ngai 2004: 2). Among transnational children, *alien citizens* are often U.S. citizens who are dependents of undocumented migrant parents or caregivers, and the construction of a citizen as "alien" happens precisely because of one's family relations. The experiences of *alien citizens* are varied, ranging from forced expulsion from the nation when a parent is deported to situations in which parents choose to have U.S. citizen children raised in Mexico because of the constant threat of their own deportation within the United States.

Like Emilio, U.S. citizen children are often forced to "return" to their parents' country of origin when parents are deported. Children are in a tenuous position in the United States should a parent be deported; they may be taken into state custody or deported themselves, even when the child is a U.S. citizen. Recent deportation cases around the country raise questions about the rights of children when the state apprehends parents, particularly when children are very young and/or U.S. citizens (e.g., Capps et al. 2007; Chaudry et al. 2010). For example, very young children have been detained in ICE facilities (e.g., Carroll and Althaus 2011), de facto deported although as U.S. citizens they cannot legally be removed from the nation by ICE officials (e.g., Byrd 2010; Dolnick 2011), and separated from parents as infants when their parents are detained (e.g., Preston 2007).

Among families from Mexico, the notion of "return" for U.S. citizen children is indeed problematic. Because of their parents' undocumented status in the United States, the majority of these children have never actually been to Mexico, and the experience of being what is essentially a "deported U.S. citizen"—itself a curious concept—brings significant challenges. One teenager, Josefa, had been in Mexico for several months when we met at the weekly market near the rancho. When Josefa spotted me, the only *gringa* in the crowd, she immediately approached me and introduced herself in English. She told me that she had been born in the United States and was eager to return to her home in Arizona, where her studies and social life were. She described how youth in the rancho treated her. "I don't think they understand me," she explained. "And, honestly, I don't understand them either. It is so boring here! I can't wait to go back."

A recent report by the Urban Institute and the National Council of La Raza estimates that two-thirds of children with deported parents are U.S. citizens (Capps et al. 2007)—if deported, parents have few options but to take their children with them, resulting in both the symbolic and actual "alien-ation" (Coutin 2000) that underscores contingent citizenship. Children of apprehended or deported parents are "alien" explicitly through their family relations and by virtue of their age. In an article in the *New York Times,* spokespersons from a government agency (Immigration and Customs Enforcement) and an anti-immigrant group (FAIR [Federation for American Immigration Reform]) stated that U.S. citizen children must pay the price for their parents' "criminal acts" (Preston 2007), articulating how easily "illegality" is transferred from parent to child.

The experiences of minor U.S. citizens whose parents are undocumented migrants serve as an example of the complexities that emerge from multiple layers of rights, as well as the denial of rights, among transnational subjects. One prominent unresolved issue is the right of these U.S. citizens to live in the United States. The predicament for U.S. citizen children with parents who are unauthorized migrants is that they cannot petition for their parents until they are twenty-one years old. While in the abstract all U.S. citizens are free to live in the United States, the actual lived experiences of such children are more complicated. Although the Immigration and Nationality Act of 1965 did include a provision through which minor U.S. citizens could petition for their undocumented migrant parents, the program was relatively brief—only those born between July 1, 1968, and December 31, 1976, were eligible (De Genova 1999: 448–49). Today's calls to rescind citizenship as birthright to the U.S.-born children of undocumented migrants or to deport U.S. citizens whose parents are unauthorized migrants reflect striking shifts in the political climate over the past several decades, and underscore the vulnerability of young migrants, both documented and undocumented.

Many U.S. citizen children go to Mexico, often for the first time, if their parents are deported. In addition, unauthorized migrants are increasingly sending their U.S. citizen children to Mexico to live for extended periods, a kind of preemptive strategy to avoid the threat of deportation and its potentially devastating impact on children and families. For example, when Nina sent her U.S. citizen children to live in the rancho with their grandparents for several years, it was because of her own position as an unauthorized migrant (see chap. 6). Nina said that she was pleased that the children were able to study in Mexico and experience life on the rancho, but she missed them immensely and ultimately chose to reunite the family in the United States. Despite her decision, however, she still considers sending the children to Mexico once more, especially because she feels increasingly vulnerable in the United States.

Preemptive relocations of children by undocumented migrant parents highlight the state's penetration into family life. By extending "illegality" to all family members, including U.S. citizens, the state effectively targets each member of mixed-status families. The state's presence in family life has profound implications for the nation and how the nation defines membership and belonging. Forced relocation of U.S. citizen children, for example, essentially converts U.S. citizens with undocumented (im)migrant family members into de facto partial members or even nonmembers of the nation. As contingent citizens, these U.S. citizen children are indeed what Ngai calls "impossible subjects" (Ngai 2004). The state's production of "illegal aliens" is a process through which the rights of citizens—and at times citizenship itself—are sacrificed with disturbing ease.

Citizen Aliens: Not Here, Here

"What can I do to protect my children?" Alma asked in a hushed voice. We were attending a community meeting to address immigrant issues, and when Alma learned that I was an academic working with transnational Mexicans, she approached me for advice. "My family, we are undocumented, and there are so many risks." Alma moved closer and asked again, "What can be done? Anything?" Alma's questions carry an urgency to act. And, yet, amid ongoing debates about immigration reform, discussion of a return to an extensive guestworker program, and efforts to pass the DREAM Act (Development, Relief and Education for Alien Minors Act, a proposed bill that would grant U.S. permanent residency to unauthorized migrants who entered the United States as minors), legislative action and substantive change seem a long way off. Meanwhile, state actions are seemingly everywhere, surrounding, or in the words of one father, "suffocating," (im)migrant families.

Informed by and building on Ngai's analysis, I propose the notion of *citizen aliens*—that is, undocumented migrant children who, in particular circumstances, are de facto members of the nation. Clearly, they are not state-recognized citizens, and they are arguably excluded more often than included. Still, the reality is that transnational children and youth live in neighborhoods, attend school, work, shop, eat out, go to parks and public spaces, and interact with community members each day. Alma's two eldest children, twenty-year-old Fidel and nineteen-year-old Iliana, are both undocumented, having lived in the United States without papers for nearly ten years. Both young people, however, are attending college on scholarships—majoring in biology and literature—and working in the community:

Fidel is cleaning offices and Iliana is a nanny for a suburban family with three young children. They are active in several groups on campus, and their weekends are spent socializing with friends, relationships established over the past decade. And yet, their futures are defined by profound uncertainty. Alma is encouraging her children to return to Mexico after they graduate, or to seek employment with an international company. "What should they do?" asked Alma. "Stay here and work cleaning houses?" The experiences of Iliana and Fidel demonstrate how, as young people age, the effects of illegality become more prominent (Gonzales 2011).

Within undocumented and mixed-status families, the U.S. state's construction of illegality permeates daily life: threat of deportation, the inability to move freely, and lack of access to health care and education affect all family members, and particularly children, regardless of one's individual legal position. Consider the experiences of Oscar, a young man who was deported weeks after his eighteenth birthday during an ICE raid at his place of employment. According to friends who attended high school with him, after Oscar was apprehended, he was sent to a detention center in Arizona and then sent "back" to Mexico. Oscar came to the United States from Mexico as an infant and has no recollection of his hometown. His day-to-day life in the United States was no different from that of his U.S. citizen siblings or cousins, and, again highlighting some of the challenges in delíneating immigrant generations (see chap. 6), his "return" to Mexico is comparable in many ways to the forced relocation of U.S. citizen children when their parents are deported. The state creates him as "alien" though his de facto membership in the nation is undeniable.

Individual rights are indeed threatened, but as I have outlined, the state's maneuvers that define (il)legality and status play out among families, impacting the well-being of children regardless of their legal status. The categorization of individual migrants as "aliens" who are "legal" or "illegal," and the many state actions intertwined with the production of (il)legality, arguably impact all members of transnational migrant families. The Melina family further illustrates this point. After living in Albuquerque for nearly twelve years, the Melina family faced the deportation of their husband and father, Cristo. Cristo's wife, Lety, returned to the rancho with three of their children, ages thirteen, ten, and six. Their thirteen-year-old son was born in Mexico and does not have papers, but the two youngest children are U.S. citizens. Although they are unauthorized migrants, four of the Melina children—seventeen, twenty, twenty-two, and twenty-four years old—chose to stay in New Mexico because their lives were firmly rooted there. For example, Bella, seventeen, wants to graduate from high school, and Vito, twenty-four, is recently married and has a baby boy, a U.S. citizen. The lives of Bella, Vito, and their siblings are *not here, here*, not recognized legally by the U.S. state, and yet, concretely and undeniably situated in the United States.

The presence and absence, of such *citizen aliens*, demonstrates how the place, as both geographical location and one's position within broader communities and the nation, of young people is shifting ground. Cases in which the deportation of unauthorized youth has been deferred—such as that of Rigoberto Padilla, a student at the University of Illinois-Chicago (Preston 2009)—underscore the complex relationship between the state and individuals who cannot be neatly slotted into legal categories of "citizen" or "alien." State agents recognize, at least in part, the problematic elements of the state's own system of categorization. Similarly, a documentary series by Latino USA titled "American Dreamer: Sam's Story" features a young man who has lived in the United States without authorization since he was a very young child; the program articulates the difficulties situating his membership within the nation. When asked, "Are you a citizen of the U.S. or a citizen of Mexico?" Sam is unsure how to reply. "I don't know," he says. "I almost feel like E.T.— alien" (February 19, 2010, Latino USA). This notion, that young people are both in-between and outside of legal categories, destabilizes the categories themselves, even as such classification by the state takes on renewed strength.

The State of (Re)production

When a previous neighbor, an elderly woman, learned that I conduct research with transnational Mexicans, she, like Alma, pulled me close and whispered in my ear with a sense of urgency. Yet her message was quite distinct from Alma's concerns about how best to protect her children. Instead, my neighbor wanted to know how might we protect our nation from all these migrants and their many children? "This used to be the Mexicans' land . . . but they want it back," she warned as her eyes widened. "By having so many children, they plan to repopulate the [U.S.] southwest. That is what you should study." Her fears reflect the broader contradiction that informs state policies and practices, a production-reproduction tension that is intertwined with U.S. immigration policy. The nation depends on and encourages migrant labor, yet immigration policies often reflect the state's desire to maintain reproduction outside of state boundaries (see Chavez 2001, 2008; Rodríguez 1996; Shandy 2008; Wilson 2000, 2006). State policies push family life outside the borders of the nation-state, and kinship ties both threaten and are co-opted by the state. It is from this nexus of state-family-individual that contradictory discourses and experiences emerge.

The state impossibly expects migrants to be simultaneously *here* and *not here*. Certainly, the state formally and informally solicits migrants to be *here*. As scholars have repeatedly shown, "undocumented migrations are, indeed, preeminently labor migrations" (De Genova 2002: 422). Yet the state also excludes migrants, constructing them as *not here*, especially through its interactions with migrant families and processes of reproduction, ranging from the birth and care of children to forms of social reproduction and the continuity or maintenance of communal ties. The state brings migrants, as individual laborers, into the nation even as it expels families and communities. Both history and current debates show that the nation desires detached individuals or, curiously, even parts of individuals—bracero, for example, derives from the Spanish word *brazos* or "arms"—to fulfill labor needs. Individual, temporary labor migrants fulfill the productive, economic needs of the state and its members.

In public discourse, the migrant is often represented as a solitary subject and/or part of a threatening mass of humans moving across the border (Chavez 2001, 2008; Santa Ana 2002; Sassen 1999). This contradictory representation is perpetuated by state actions aimed at addressing the perceived "wave" of transmigrants specifically by disciplining individual subjects. However, both representations—migrant as individual and migrants as part of an ominous flow—serve to construct production as detached from reproduction. When migrants are perceived as individual, autonomous laborers, criminals breaking the law, there is an explicit denial of children; migrants are cast as the antithesis of hardworking and loyal members of families who go north precisely in an effort to create a sense of well-being for kin (Boehm 2008a). On the other hand, the depiction of migrants as part of a dangerous collective presents an exaggerated view of reproduction and its effects (Chavez 2008).

Children and youth are at the center of this production-reproduction predicament, a dilemma for the state but especially for young people and families. There is a perceived risk to the state and nation that children ostensibly pose, perpetuated by a narrative in which Mexicans or Latinos present a "reproductive threat, altering the demographic makeup of the nation" (Chavez 2008: 51). This is a gendered discourse that especially situates mothers and their children as a risk to citizenship itself (Chavez 2008). Furthermore, public discourse expresses ambivalence about (im)migrant children and the children of (im)migrants: young people are perceived as both individuals in need of the state's protection and a collective threat to the nation and its members (Terrio 2008; Uehling 2008). At the nexus of production and reproduction, the state's power to penetrate intimate lives plays out in specific ways among children and youth.

The everyday lives of migrant families and children call for a move beyond consideration of migrants in these contradictory ways, to understanding children—and indeed all migrants—as inherently embedded within particular families and social networks. Clearly no individual exists without attachment to others. Nor do migrants make up a homogenous collective or mass, a community whose experiences are always common or unified; indeed, "there are no hermetically sealed communities of undocumented migrants" (De Genova 2002: 422). While transnational Mexicans would agree that their migrations are labor migrations, they also understand labor migrations to be inextricably tied to family life. Mexicans migrate and work to provide for their families, partners, and children. Simplistic representations of migrants as detached individuals or dangerous waves systematically dismiss children and youth as actors at the center of migration processes, and essentially render children invisible. In this frame, children are conceptually—legally and in popular discourse—*here* and *not here*, underscoring the bind of transnational (re)production.

In excluding individual family members—along lines of gender and generation—the state creates a predicament for itself, for families, and ultimately, for young people. For members of undocumented and mixed-status families, inclusion within the nation is "simultaneously a social reality and a legal impossibility" (Ngai 2004: 4). The state's desire to recruit laborers who are disconnected from partners, parents, siblings, and children cannot be actualized. The everyday lives of Mexicans challenge the state's narrow construction of migrants as solely laborers and as disconnected individuals. For its part, the U.S. state creates a situation in which all members of families are defined, and often excluded, through the status of individuals. For the state, a child who is an unauthorized migrant—or who has family members who are unauthorized within the United States—is both "a person who cannot be and a problem that cannot be solved" (Ngai 2004: 5). Transnational children and their families are quite literally "caught in the crossfire" (Grossberg 2005), wedged in a conundrum with few solutions.

By constructing undocumented migrants, both adults and children, as paradoxically *not here, here*, the nation-state maintains an expendable workforce, and by situating migrant children—particularly U.S. citizens—as *here, not here*, the state aims to ensure that reproduction, the care of children, and family life take place outside the boundaries of the nation. Of course, the state's vision of maintaining migrant children and families outside of national borders is only partially realized. Although they are excluded, legally and through state practices, migrant children and their families are undeniably *here*. And still, U.S. policies and practices are likely to intensify state presence in transnational family life, often locating migrant children and youth, even U.S. nationals, *there*. While the experience of being *here–not here* is intensified among young people, the experiences of children and youth underscore the contingent character of citizenship for people of all ages within transnational communities.

Transnational Futures

"They are *hijos de mojados* [children of undocumented migrants, literally "children of wetbacks"], you know," Perla said of her grandchildren.[2] The majority of Perla's grandchildren—the *hijos* to whom she referred—are U.S. citizens, born in the United States. Yet several of Perla's children—those she called the *mojados*—are undocumented. "What will it be like for these children, these *hijos de mojados*?" she wondered aloud. Perla had talked with me many times before about the dangers her adult children face in the United States, and I knew from our conversations that she constantly worried about their safety. She paused, and then contemplated her grandchildren's future, "I imagine it will be quite different for them than it is for their parents, don't you think?"

Perla's speculation about the future of her children and grandchildren underscores the importance of looking at (re)production among transnational families over time. These are, indeed, processes-in-the-making, an uncertain trajectory that is unfolding as Mexican migrants build families within two nation-states and as U.S. immigration laws change with frequency. While the Mexican migrants I work with do not go to the United States to have children who will be U.S. citizens—in fact, over the course of my research no parent has expressed their motivations to migrate in these terms—members of the community do recognize how the paths of children with birthright U.S. citizenship will differ vastly from that of children born in Mexico. It is likely that the next generation will be slotted into a class system ordered by U.S. legal status, an emergent hierarchy of *alien citizens* and *citizen aliens* that could intensify difference and inequalities. The U.S. state's system of legal status is indeed shaping the lives of young people and (re)constituting family in a transnational space.

Perla recently became a great-grandmother to a U.S. citizen with parents and grandparents who are undocumented migrants. The interconnected processes of ongoing undocumented migration and a rise in the number of children born to parents without authorization to be in the United States will continue to impact transnational Mexicans, and have significant implications for the future trajectories of transnational families. Regardless of their status in the United States, Mexican (im)migrants are controlled by the U.S. state but still building lives and families outside of state control. Transnational Mexicans, and especially transnational children, live on the margins of two countries. By penetrating, disrupting, and at times tearing apart families, the state maintains its power, and transnational Mexicans continue to exist *here* and *not here*, "from neither here nor there."

Conclusion

Ni de Aquí, Ni de Allá/
From Neither Here nor There

"I wander about . . . I am from neither here nor there [*ni de aquí, ni de allá*]!"
Ofelia stated emphatically, and then she began to laugh. Ofelia was recounting
her many migrations between Mexico and the United States, and the bureaucratic process through which she was attempting to secure U.S. permanent
residency. She had just returned to the rancho from Albuquerque where she
had filed necessary paperwork for residency through her eldest son. When we
spoke, she was waiting for her appointment to be scheduled, and in the meantime, she had been assigned an identification number and documents granting
her permission to travel back and forth. She said that she was worried about an
event that took place many years earlier, when she was detained by U.S. Border
Patrol agents as she waded across the Rio Grande. As Ofelia told me, "They
caught me. I was caught [she used the verb *"pescar"* which means "to fish"]."
Standing in the river that separates and joins Mexico and the United States,
Ofelia was, quite literally, in a space that is, as discussed in the previous chapter, *here–not here*, and in her words, "from neither here nor there."

Ofelia wondered how the apprehension might affect the process of becoming a resident. She explained that it is very important for her to get permanent residency because with a green card she will be able to visit her children
and grandchildren in the United States without difficulties. She does not like
living in the United States and much prefers Mexico, but she wants to be able
to travel to the States because the majority of her family lives there. She said
that she does not intend to become a U.S. citizen, at least not right away; for
now, U.S. permanent residency will be sufficient, enabling her to move back
and forth. Ofelia is among the few for whom there is this pathway to legalization; she does have a chance to be recognized by the state as a member of the
nation. But Ofelia's situation is unique because she has papers: most of the
current migrants from the rancho do not.

While Victor (see Introduction) frames belonging as "from both sides" and Lucía (see chap. 2) describes herself as divided—"half there, half here"—and with ties to two countries, Ofelia portrays herself as "from neither here nor there," a migrant without a home, wandering about, from neither the United States nor Mexico and yet living within both countries. This is a telling description of migrants' relationship to the U.S. state as they live within a transnational circuit. Ofelia's experiences demonstrate how the state has a strong presence, and yet, she has also circumvented state control. Indeed, she successfully crossed the border several times without documents and lived for extended periods in the United States, and hopes to continue to divide her time between San Marcos and Albuquerque. The fact that she feels excluded even as she moves toward legal status and permanent residency is indicative of the exclusionary dimensions of state categories.

Although migrants strategically use state policies and practices if and when they are able, the state's power has far-reaching effects in transnational Mexicans' everyday experiences. Indeed, the production of illegality interacts with—and often shapes—the intimate exchanges of daily life, resulting in the multiple spatial and metaphorical places migrants reside. That migrants repeatedly situate themselves in both places ("from here and from there"), divided by the border ("half there, half here"), and/or between two nations ("from neither here nor there") captures these shifting locations of intimate spaces and states of (il)legality. A significant contradiction in the lives of transnational Mexicans is the fact that within a transnational space, and yet living in two autonomous nation-states, (im)migrants exercise independence even as they are subjected to intense controls.

On the one hand, transnationals have added flexibility—that is, in particular circumstances, they have the ability to take actions that elude the state. Aihwa Ong's notion of "flexible citizenship" (Ong 1999), which she defines as the strategies of individuals "seeking to both circumvent *and* benefit from different nation-state regimes" (Ong 1999: 112), is useful here. On the other hand, for transnational subjects, whether documented or undocumented, living in multiple nation-states can constrict flexibility, curbing their rights and limiting their ability to maneuver vis-à-vis a state or states: "although increasingly able to escape localization by state authorities, traveling subjects are never free of regulations set by state power" (Ong 1999: 19–20). Given the political and historical context within which Mexican nationals migrate—or not—to the United States, their position vis-à-vis the U.S. state is in many ways the converse of flexible citizenship; theirs is a kind of *inflexible citizenship* or contingent membership that may be compromised explicitly through gender and family relations and according to age, even for U.S. citizens and permanent residents. This is the conundrum that produces the "discontents" (Sassen 1998) of globalization and shapes the everyday lives of transmigrants.

The transnational Mexicans described throughout the book experience what Rouse has termed a "chronic, contradictory transnationalism" (Rouse 1992: 46). This transnationalism is, without question, contradictory. Many of the contradictions that emerge from transnational migration as it is enacted through intimate relationships have been the focus of this book: how families transcend and are divided by the U.S.-Mexico border, how gender subjectivities are transforming and being reasserted, how gendered power relations among transmigrants operate both within and outside of the force of U.S. state, and how age intersects with U.S. immigration status. An analysis of such inconsistencies, discrepancies, uncertainties, and ambiguities—in short, the substance of everyday experience—can actually add clarity to understandings of transnational processes as well as the character of and motivations for migration itself.

This transnationalism is also chronic in that it is persistent, ongoing, continuous—although chronic, however, it is never uniform, homogenous, or predictable. For centuries, the extended U.S.-Mexico borderlands have been characterized by diverse migrations. This book, therefore, is situated in a particular historical moment and provides a snapshot of transnational processes that will continue to alter and transform (see Kearney 1995: 355–56). Although I have outlined the many ways that the border is a profound barrier in the lives of transmigrants (especially in chaps. 3, 5, and 7), transnational ties will continue to be strong among future generations, albeit in new permutations, and migrants will continue to be "at home" in transnational spaces (Hess 2009: 212). Such cross-border trajectories—this chronic, contradictory transnationalism—call for longitudinal, binational and multi-sited ethnographic study, research that is locally situated to capture the diversity of experiences of migrant communities.

Intimacy and Illegality

Among the most persistent contradictions in the lives of transnational migrants are those at intersection of intimacy and the production of illegality. Emic power imbalances—along lines of family position, age, and gender—are ever present in Mexican lives, and still these supposedly intimate relations are always overlaid by state power and the U.S. state's categorization of migrants, problematizing the conceptual division between state actions and the everyday experiences of women, men, girls, and boys, as members of families and across generations. Transnational migrants are embedded in relationships as partners, parents, siblings, and children, and must be considered as such in analyses of transnationality. Mexican (im)migrants experience migrations in profoundly different ways, based on complex and interconnected positionalities and aspects of the self, including—though not limited to—gender, age, generation, class position, legal status within the United States, access to resources, race/ethnicity, sexuality, marital status, and kin relations.

A primary sphere is that of family and relatedness. Mexican (im)migrant families and communities, living within and across two nation-states, experience both fluidity and divisions, and their lives both transcend and are separated by this international division. An analysis of family reunification makes the effects and inconsistencies of legal frameworks transparent. "Family reunification" is itself compromised through a U.S. legal framework that ostensibly aims to bring family members together. One area that will be of importance for future study is the growing number of mixed-status families living in the United States and transnationally (Passel and Cohn 2009). Such configurations of family have significant implications for how the U.S. state includes and excludes members, how U.S. immigration reform might be structured, and the rights of U.S. citizens, both children and adults, within mixed-status families and partnerships.

Gender, also, is a primary axis of power shaping transborder movement, a set of relationships that are, again, repeatedly shaped by constructions of illegality. Such "gendered geographies of power" (Mahler and Pessar 2001a) play out in specific sites and within particular relations. While manhood is created explicitly through movement and migration, women are often constrained by closure and stasis, processes that may be enforced or even concretized because of U.S. immigration laws, practices along the U.S.-Mexico border, and growing anti-immigrant sentiment within the United States. However, gendered patterns of migration are never absolute. For example, as U.S. deportations of Mexican nationals increase, gendered exchanges will continue to shift. Deportations—that like migrations are masculinized—are likely to direct and disrupt future gendered migration flows, resulting in emergent feminized migrations and new configurations of family.

It is arguably among the next generation that the effects of "illegality" are most potent. While the flexibility or range of possibility for individual agents are shaped by migrants' own understandings of authority and power, particularly those at the intersection of age and gender, the state's presence is strong in the lives of young people. Cultural meanings and orders attached to age interact with and are recast through U.S. definitions of national membership, resulting in a kind of contingent citizenship. Shifting notions of belonging and exclusion impact, to varying degrees, all transnational Mexicans, but such processes come into relief when considering the lives of infants, children, and youth as they move, do not move, or are placed by caregivers in specific geographical spaces throughout the U.S.-Mexico transnation. As discussed earlier, within transnational communities there is a growing number of U.S. citizen children whose parents are unauthorized migrants. While the current residence of such children and youth is determined by the migration trajectories of their families, in the future these children will be able to "go and come [*ir y venir*]" more easily than their parents. It remains to be seen if these individuals will be among the multiple-passport holders identified by Ong (1999), to what extent they will maintain significant ties to Mexico (Smith 2002, 2006), how they will structure their lives within a transnational space, and in what ways such processes will be gendered.

Transnational Mexicans—regardless of their status in the United States—are building lives and families outside of state control and yet they are repeatedly restricted by the nation-state. The everyday experiences of transnational families underscore contradictions within the state itself: even as transnational Mexicans challenge and circumvent state power, the experiences of Mexican migrant families uncover the strong hold of the state. Ofelia's portrayal of herself as "from neither here nor there" accurately describes Mexican (im)migrants who live on the margins of two countries—a position that draws attention to both the potency, and permeability, of state power. The question of who will protect the rights of transnational Mexicans—as individuals, as males and females of all ages, and as members of families and larger communities—remains unanswered.

It is likely that in the future transnational Mexicans will live transcending, and yet divided by, the U.S.-Mexico border. Mexican (im)migrants will continue to practice and experience transnational lives that are—as they describe—"from both sides," "half there, half here," and persistently, "from neither here nor there." The unjust realities of lives that are between here and there can guide us to reimagine and create a world where state power and the often arbitrary categories linked to immigration status do not have a dehumanizing effect. Indeed, the most intimate of relationships depend on it.

Postscript: Caught

As Gerardo sat at the Department of Motor Vehicles (DMV), he wondered why the renewal of his auto registration would take so much time. Gerardo had heard that wait times could be long at this office, so he stayed put. But after several hours, five ICE agents appeared, arrested Gerardo, and took him into custody, first at a county jail and then at a federal immigration detention center hours away from his home. At the time of the arrest, Gerardo had lived in the United States for nearly two decades without papers, after migrating as a teenager. He had children who were U.S. citizens, and he had made a life for himself and his family in the United States. Before that day, Gerardo had actually expressed fear about going to the DMV, and was hesitant to do so, because of rumors circulating that ICE agents were arresting undocumented migrants there. Ironically, he thought it was important to follow the laws of the United States and so he went ahead with registering his car. Gerardo's fears were actualized through his experience of the everyday; the seemingly mundane act of registering his vehicle, and, poignantly, what he understood to be his duty as a responsible community member, resulted in this event that changed his life course. He was detained, caught by ICE agents, and, ultimately, trapped by a legal system in need of reform.

Like Ofelia, who described being caught by U.S. Border Patrol agents (see Conclusion), Gerardo, too, was and is "caught" on several levels. Of course, Gerardo was caught in a literal sense, arrested, and then detained, unable to communicate with family and friends. He was found to be living in the United States without papers, like nearly 12 million other migrants, although not by chance. Gerardo's arrest was one of many actions that are taking place at the local level, arguably a patterned or systematic process through which the jurisdiction of city, county, and in this case, state government becomes blurred with efforts by federal immigration agencies. In this way, Gerardo was caught in an encounter that is part of widespread and growing government efforts that often seem, oddly, disparate or even disorganized, and yet are highly orchestrated.

In addition, Gerardo is caught or "stuck" (Stephen 2007: 309) in a state of limbo, waiting for an outcome that seems at once unpredictable and nearly certain (Boehm 2009). Gerardo is awaiting trial to determine whether he will be deported. His attorney has counseled the family that the chances of avoiding deportation are extremely slim. The 1996 Illegal Immigration Reform and Immigrant Responsibility Act and the events of 9/11 have set the stage for today's control of undocumented migration. The U.S. crackdown on unauthorized migration in recent years has been implemented through an increasingly militarized border (Cornelius 2006), federal immigration raids in locations throughout the United States (e.g., Capps et al. 2007), deportations of undocumented migrants with U.S. citizen children (e.g., Preston 2007), state laws and local ordinances and practices aimed at curbing undocumented migration (Cave 2008), and a growing number of U.S. permanent residents who are being denied citizenship or even deported during the naturalization process (Preston 2008) or when filing for a change in immigration status.[1]

The United States is currently experiencing what may be considered an age of deportation (see Boehm 2011c): over the past decades, deportations of foreign nationals from the United States have been on the rise (U.S. Department of Homeland Security 2008: 95). Mexican nationals make up the largest number of individuals identified by the U.S. Department of Homeland Security as "deportable" (U.S. Department of Homeland Security 2008: 92), and deportations are increasing among transnational Mexicans, affecting families and communities in both the United States and Mexico. When I first went to the rancho in 2001, I knew no deportees. A decade later, dozens of people from San Marcos and neighboring towns have been deported, and far more have returned to Mexico because of deportations of family members.

Deportations and deportability are having a profound effect on the intimate lives described throughout this book. Gerardo's family, for example, is anticipating a likely "return" to Mexico as a result of his deportation, although Gerardo's children are U.S. citizens who have never been to his country of origin. Families, and especially children, experience intense disruption as a result of deportation, perhaps even more so than in cases of transnational migration. While migration separates couples and families, it does benefit transnational Mexicans: the sacrifices of family members on both sides of the border typically result in the support of families. Raids, detentions, and deportations, on the other hand, nearly always leave transnational Mexicans in emotionally and financially precarious situations. In addition, as families negotiate this age of deportation, gender subjectivities and relations continue to shift, and gendered inequalities are likely to be reinforced. An increase in deportations of primarily men has left families divided, has resulted in children (unauthorized migrants and U.S. citizens) living in the United States without their parents, is redirecting gendered migration flows, and is a form of cross-border movement that is, once again, reconfiguring transnational lives.

This unpredictability extends to ways that U.S.-Mexico transnationality will unfold in upcoming years. In the current political climate, it is difficult to imagine when or if comprehensive immigration reform will take place in the United States. Among North American leaders, diplomatic discussions about drug violence, climate change, and economic crisis have eclipsed attention to (im)migration (e.g., Thompson and Lacey 2009)—a striking omission given the millions of people affected by unauthorized migration throughout the region. Within the United States, public sentiment and political actions are moving toward increased restrictions federally, within states, and in local contexts. Deportations have risen under President Obama, states have passed increasingly stringent immigration laws, and the Secure Communities program and 287(g) agreements—"law enforcement partnerships" (U.S. Immigration and Customs Enforcement)—between local law enforcement agencies and ICE are expanding. Deportations are on the rise, as are the ripple effects of U.S. laws and practices.

Finally, Gerardo, Ofelia, and millions of other transnational Mexicans are indeed "caught" in a persistent place of liminality. While the embodiment of living "from neither here nor there" may be particularly evident among unauthorized migrants and young people with or without papers, this state of being aptly captures the status of community members living on both sides of the border and people of all ages. Transnational Mexicans are collectively caught in a legal system that is broken, in a social space that is in-between, but potentially within a borderlands of possibility. It is perhaps in the liminal places between here and there, these "tiny cracks" (Tsing 2005: 267) or spaces "beyond" (Bhabha 1994: 4), that a view of imagined future trajectories is possible. We are at a threshold of something yet to come, the next chapter in the story of unauthorized migration in the twenty-first century. May it be a time when U.S. immigration policies reflect the everyday lives of transnational Mexicans who are, in fact, "from both sides."

Notes

INTRODUCTION

1. Aspects of this discussion and Ofelia's experiences (with the pseudonym "Estrella") were previously published in "'*Ir y Venir*': Historias Transnacionales, Trayectorias Determinadas por Genero" in *¡Yo Soy de San Luis Potosí! . . . con un Pie en Estados Unidos*, ed. Fernando Saúl Alanis Enciso (San Luis Potosí, S.L.P., Mexico: Instituto Nacional de Migración-Centro de Estudios Migratorios, SEGOB, El Colegio de San Luis, A.C. Porrúa, IPICYT, 2008), (see Boehm 2008b).

CHAPTER 2

1. This section draws on "'From Both Sides': (Trans)nationality, Citizenship, and Belonging among Mexican Immigrants to the United States," in *Rethinking Refuge and Displacement, Selected Papers on Refugees and Immigrants,* vol. 8, 2001, ed. Elzbieta M. Goździak and Dianna J. Shandy (Arlington, VA: American Anthropological Association–Committee on Refugees and Immigrants, 2001), (see Boehm 2001).

CHAPTER 3

1. Sections of this chapter were previously published in an *Anthropological Quarterly* article "'For My Children': Constructing Family and Navigating the State in the U.S.-Mexico Transnation" (Boehm 2008a).

CHAPTER 4

1. A version of this chapter was previously published in a *Latin American Perspectives* article "'Now I Am a Man and a Woman!': Gendered Moves and Migrations in a Transnational Mexican Community" (Boehm 2008c). It also draws from "'*Ir y Venir*'" in *¡Yo Soy de San Luis Potosí!,* ed. Fernando Saúl Alanis Enciso (Boehm 2008b).

CHAPTER 5

1. This section draws on "*Deseos y Dolores*: Mapping Desire, Suffering, and (Dis)loyalty within Transnational Partnerships," *International Migration* (Boehm 2011a).

CHAPTER 6

1. Sections of this chapter draw on "'For My Children': Constructing Family and Navigating the State in the U.S.-Mexico Transnation," *Anthropological Quarterly* (Boehm 2008a).

CHAPTER 7

1. A version of this chapter was previously published as "Here/Not Here: Contingent Citizenship and Transnational Mexican Children," in *Everyday Ruptures: Children, Youth, and Migration in Global Perspective*, ed. Cati Coe, Rachel Reynolds, Deborah A. Boehm, Julia Meredith Hess, and Heather Rae-Espinoza (Vanderbilt University Press, 2011), (Boehm 2011b).

2. This section was originally published in "'For My Children': Constructing Family and Navigating the State in the U.S.-Mexico Transnation," *Anthropological Quarterly* (Boehm 2008a).

POSTSCRIPT

1. Aspects of this discussion and Gerardo's experiences (with the pseudonym "Felipe") were first published in "'¿Quien Sabe?': Deportation and Temporality among Transnational Mexicans," *Urban Anthropology and Studies of Cultural Systems and World Economic Development* (Boehm 2009).

Bibliography

Abu-Lughod, Lila. 1999. *Writing Women's Worlds*. Berkeley: University of California Press.

Alarcón, Norma, Caren Kaplan, and Minoo Moallem. 1999. "Introduction: Between Woman and Nation." In *Between Woman and Nation: Nationalisms, Transnational Feminisms, and the State*, edited by Caren Kaplan, Norma Alarcón, and Minoo Moallem, 1–16. Durham, NC: Duke University Press.

Alexander, M. Jacqui, and Chandra Talpade Mohanty, eds. 1997. *Feminist Genealogies, Colonial Legacies, Democratic Futures*. New York: Routledge.

Almaguer, Tomas. 1994. *Racial Fault Lines: The Historical Origins of White Supremacy in California*. Berkeley: University of California Press.

Alonso, Ana María. 1994. "The Politics of Space, Time, and Substance: State Formation, Nationalism, and Ethnicity." *Annual Review of Anthropology* 23: 379–405.

———. 1995. *Thread of Blood: Colonialism, Revolution, and Gender on Mexico's Northern Frontier*. Tucson: University of Arizona Press.

Alvarez, Robert R. Jr. 1987. *Familia: Migration and Adaptation in Baja and Alta California, 1800–1975*. Berkeley: University of California Press.

———. 1995. "The Mexican-U.S. Border: The Making of an Anthropology of Borderlands." *Annual Review of Anthropology* 24: 447–70.

Anderson, Benedict. 1991. *Imagined Communities: Reflections on the Origin and Spread of Nationalism*. London: Verso.

Anzaldúa, Gloria. 1987. *Borderlands/La Frontera: The New Mestiza*. San Francisco: Aunt Lute Books.

Appadurai, Arjun. 1989. "On Moving Targets." *Public Culture* 2 (1): i–iv.

———. 1996. *Modernity at Large: Cultural Dimensions of Globalization*. Minneapolis: University of Minnesota Press.

———. 2006. *Fear of Small Numbers: An Essay on the Geography of Anger*. Durham, NC: Duke University Press.

Aretxaga, Begoña. 2003. "Maddening States." *Annual Review of Anthropology* 32: 393–410.

Bailey, Adrian J. 2009. "Viewpoint: On Transnational Migration, Deepening Vulnerabilities, and the Challenge of Membership." *Migration Letters* 6 (1): 75–82.

Basch, Linda, Nina Glick Schiller, and Christina Szanton Blanc. 1994. *Nations Unbound: Transnational Projects and the Deterritorialized Nation-State*. New York: Gordon and Breach.

Basso, Keith H. 1996. *Wisdom Sits in Places: Landscape and Language among the Western Apache*. Albuquerque: University of New Mexico Press.

Bauböck, Rainer. 1994. *Transnational Citizenship: Membership and Rights in International Migration*. Brookfield, VT: E. Elgar.

Behar, Ruth, and Deborah A. Gordon, eds. 1995. *Women Writing Culture*. Berkeley: University of California Press.

Besserer, Federico. 1998. "A Space of View: Transnational Spaces and Perspectives." Transnationalism: An Exchange of Theoretical Perspectives from Latin American, Africanist, and Asian Anthropology, ICCCR, University of Manchester, U.K.

Bever, Sandra Weinstein. 2002. "Migration and the Transformation of Gender Roles and Hierarchies in Yucatan." *Urban Anthropology and Studies of Cultural Systems and World Economic Development* 31 (2): 199–230.

Bhabha, Homi K., 1994. *The Location of Culture*. London: Routledge.

Bhattacharjee, Anannya. 2006. "The Public/Private Mirage: Mapping Homes and Undomesticating Violence Work in the South Asian Immigrant Community." In *The Anthropology of the State: A Reader*, edited by Aradhana Sharma and Akhil Gupta, 337–56. Oxford: Blackwell Publishing.

Bjerén, Gunilla. 1997. "Gender and Reproduction." In *International Migration, Immobility and Development: Multidisciplinary Perspectives*, edited by Tomas Hammar, Grete Brochmann, Kristof Tamas, and Thomas Faist, 219–46. Oxford: Berg.

Boehm, Deborah A. 2001. "'From Both Sides': (Trans)nationality, Citizenship, and Belonging among Mexican Immigrants to the United States." In *Rethinking Refuge and Displacement, Selected Papers on Refugees and Immigrants, Vol. 8, 2001*, edited by Elzbieta M. Goździak and Dianna J. Shandy, 111–41. Arlington, VA: American Anthropological Association, Committee on Refugees and Immigrants.

———. 2008a. "'For My Children': Constructing Family and Navigating the State in the U.S.-Mexico Transnation." *Anthropological Quarterly* 81 (4): 777–802.

———. 2008b. "'*Ir y Venir*': Historias Transnacionales, Trayectorias Determinadas por Genero." In *¡Yo Soy de San Luis Potosí! . . . con un Pie en Estados Unidos*, edited by Fernando Saúl Alanis Enciso, 93–112. Instituto Nacional de Migración-Centro de Estudios Migratorios, SEGOB, El Colegio de San Luis, A.C. Porrúa, IPICYT.

———. 2008c. "'Now I Am a Man and a Woman!': Gendered Moves and Migrations in a Transnational Mexican Community." *Latin American Perspectives* 35 (1): 16–30.

———. 2009. "'¿Quien Sabe?': Deportation and Temporality among Transnational Mexicans." *Urban Anthropology and Studies of Cultural Systems and World Economic Development* 38 (2–4): 345–74.

———. 2010. "Place Matters: Community and Spatiality at Burning Man." Proceedings of the Southwestern Anthropological Association Conference, Reno, NV.

———. 2011a. "*Deseos y Dolores*: Mapping Desire, Suffering, and (Dis)loyalty within Transnational Partnerships." *International Migration* 49(6): 95–106.

———. 2011b. "Here/Not Here: Contingent Citizenship and Transnational Mexican Children." In *Everyday Ruptures: Children, Youth, and Migration in Global Perspective*, edited by Cati Coe, Rachel Reynolds, Deborah A. Boehm, Julia Meredith Hess, and Heather Rae-Espinoza, 161–73. Nashville, TN: Vanderbilt University Press.

———. 2011c. "US-Mexico Mixed Migration in an Age of Deportation: An Inquiry into the Transnational Circulation of Violence." *Refugee Survey Quarterly* 30 (1): 1–21.

Boehm, Deborah A., and M. Bianet Castellanos, eds. 2008. "Engendering Mexican Migration: Articulating Gender, Regions, Circuits." Special Issue, *Latin American Perspectives* 35 (1).

Boehm, Deborah A., Julia Meredith Hess, Cati Coe, Heather Rae-Espinoza, and Rachel R. Reynolds. 2011. "Introduction: Children, Youth, and the Everyday Ruptures of Migration." In *Everyday Ruptures: Children, Youth, and Migration in Global Perspective,* edited by Cati Coe, Rachel Reynolds, Deborah A. Boehm, Julia Meredith Hess, and Heather Rae-Espinoza, 1–19. Nashville, TN: Vanderbilt University Press.

Bourdieu, Pierre. 1977. *Outline of a Theory of Practice.* Cambridge: Cambridge University Press.

Brennan, Denise. 2004. *What's Love Got to Do with It? Transnational Desires and Sex Tourism in the Dominican Republic.* Durham, NC: Duke University Press.

Brown, Patricia Leigh. 2009. "Invisible Immigrants, Old and Left with 'Nobody to Talk To.'" *New York Times,* August 31.

Bustamante, Mercedes Olivera, and Luis Antonio Sánchez Trujillo. n.d. "Entre la Subordinación y la Rebeldía: Hacia un Análisis de las Identidades Femeninas Encarnadas." Unpublished manuscript.

Butler, Judith. 1989. *Gender Trouble: Feminism and the Subversion of Identity.* New York: Routledge.

Byrd, Shelia. 2010. "Mexican Immigrant Gets Baby Back from State." *Sun Herald* (South Mississippi Gulf Coast), February 19.

Calavita, Kitty. 1992. *Inside the State: The Bracero Program, Immigration, and the I.N.S.* New York: Routledge.

Canclini, Néstor García. 1995. *Hybrid Cultures.* Minneapolis: University of Minnesota Press.

Cantú, Lionel. 2009. Edited by Nancy A. Naples, and Salvador Vidal-Ortiz. *The Sexuality of Migration: Border Crossings and Mexican Immigrant Men.* New York: New York University Press.

Capps, Randy, Rose Maria Castañeda, Ajay Chaudry, and Robert Santos. 2007. "Paying the Price: The Impact of Immigration Raids on America's Children." A Report by The Urban Institute. Washington DC: The National Council of La Raza.

Carroll, Susan, and Dudley Althaus. 2011. "Orphaned in Mexico, Trapped in ICE Limbo." *Houston Chronicle,* February 3.

Carsten, Janet, ed. 2000. *Cultures of Relatedness: New Approaches to the Study of Kinship.* Cambridge: Cambridge University Press.

———. 2004. *After Kinship.* Cambridge: Cambridge University Press.

Castellanos, M. Bianet. 2010. *A Return to Servitude: Maya Migration and the Tourist Trade in Cancún.* Minneapolis: University of Minnesota Press.

Castellanos, M. Bianet, and Deborah A. Boehm. 2008. "Introduction: Articulating Gender, Regions, Circuits." *Latin American Perspectives* 35 (1): 5–15.

Cave, Damien. 2008. "States Take New Tack on Illegal Immigration." *New York Times,* June 9.

Center for Comparative Immigration Studies. 2005. "Forced Migration and Human Rights in San Diego: What the Public Needs to Know—A Roundtable Discussion." Forced Migration Laboratory, Center for Comparative Immigration Studies, University of California–San Diego, La Jolla, CA.

Chaudry, Ajay, Randy Capps, Juan Manuel Pedroza, Rosa Maria Casteñeda, Robert Santos, and Molly M. Scott. 2010. "Facing Our Future: Children in the Aftermath of Immigration Enforcement." A report by the Urban Institute. Washington DC: The Urban Institute.

Chavez, Leo R. 1992. *Shadowed Lives: Undocumented Immigrants in American Society*. Fort Worth, TX: Harcourt Brace Jovanovich College Publishers.

———. 2001. *Covering Immigration: Popular Images and the Politics of the Nation*. Berkeley: University of California Press.

———. 2007. "The Condition of Illegality." *International Migration* 45 (3): 192–95.

———. 2008. *The Latino Threat: Constructing Immigrants, Citizens, and the Nation*. Stanford, CA: Stanford University Press.

Clifford, James. 1997. *Routes: Travel and Translation in the Late Twentieth Century*. Cambridge, MA: Harvard University Press.

Coe, Cati. 2008. "The Structuring of Feeling in Ghanaian Transnational Families." *City and Society* 20 (2): 222–50.

Coe, Cati, Rachel R. Reynolds, Deborah A. Boehm, Julia Meredith Hess, and Heather Rae-Espinoza, eds. 2011. *Everyday Ruptures: Children, Youth, and Migration in Global Perspective*. Nashville, TN: Vanderbilt University Press.

Cohen, Jeffrey H. 2002. "Migration and 'Stay at Homes' in Rural Oaxaca, Mexico: Local Expression of Global Outcomes." *Urban Anthropology and Studies of Cultural Systems and World Economic Development* 31 (2): 231–59.

Cohen, Jeffrey H., Bernardo Rios, and Lise Byars. 2009. "The Value, Costs, and Meaning of Transnational Migration in Rural Oaxaca, Mexico." *Migration Letters* 6 (1): 15–25.

Cohen, Jeffrey H., Leila Rodriguez, and Margaret Fox. 2008. "Gender and Migration in the Central Valleys of Oaxaca." *International Migration* 46 (1): 79–101.

Cole, Jennifer, and Deborah Durham. 2007. *Generations and Globalization: Youth, Age, and Family in the New World Economy*. Bloomington: University of Indiana Press.

———. 2008. *Figuring the Future: Globalization and the Temporalities of Children and Youth*. Santa Fe, NM: School for Advanced Research Press.

Collier, Jane, Michelle Z. Rosaldo, and Sylvia Yanagisako. 1997. "Is There a Family? New Anthropological Views." In *The Gender/Sexuality Reader: Culture, History, Political Economy*, edited by Roger N. Lancaster and Micaela Di Leonardo, 71–81. New York: Routledge.

Collier, Jane, and Sylvia Yanagisako, eds. 1987. *Gender and Kinship: Essays Toward a United Analysis*. Stanford, CA: Stanford University Press.

Constable, Nicole. 2003. *Romance on a Global Stage: Pen Pals, Virtual Ethnography, and "Mail Order" Marriages*. Berkeley: University of California Press.

———. 2004. "Changing Filipina Identities and Ambivalent Returns." In *Coming Home?: Refugees, Migrants and Those Who Stayed Behind*, edited by Lynellen D. Long and Ellen Oxfeld, 104–24. Philadelphia: University of Pennsylvania Press.

———. 2009. "The Commodification of Intimacy: Marriage, Sex, and Reproductive Labor." *Annual Review of Anthropology* 38: 49–64.

Cornelius, Wayne A. 2006. "Impacts of Border Enforcement on Unauthorized Mexican Migration to the United States." Border Battles: The U.S. Immigration Debates, Web Forum of the Social Science Research Council. http://www.ssrc.org/publications/essays/.

Cornelius, Wayne A., David Fitzgerald, Pedro Lewin Fischer, Leah Muse-Orlinoff, and Micah Gell-Redman. 2010. "Preface." In *Mexican Migration and the U.S. Economic Crisis: A Transnational Perspective*, edited by Wayne A. Cornelius, David Fitzgerald, Pedro Lewin Fischer, and Leah Muse-Orlinoff, vii–xvii. San Diego: Center for Comparative Immigration Studies, University of California–San Diego.

Coutin, Susan Bibler. 2000. *Legalizing Moves: Salvadoran Immigrants' Struggle for U.S. Residency*. Ann Arbor: University of Michigan Press.

———. 2003. "Suspension of Deportation Hearings: Racialization, Immigration, and 'Americanness.'" *Journal of Latin American Anthropology* 8 (2): 58–95.

———. 2005. "Being en Route." *American Anthropologist* 107 (2): 195–206.

———. 2007. *Nations of Emigrants: Shifting Boundaries of Citizenship in El Salvador and the United States*. Ithaca, NY: Cornell University Press.

Creed, Gerald W. 2000. "'Family Values' and Domestic Economies." *Annual Review of Anthropology* 29: 329–55.

De Genova, Nicholas. 1999. "Working the Boundaries, Making the Difference: Race and Space in Mexican Chicago." PhD diss., Department of Anthropology, University of Chicago.

———. 2002. "Migrant 'Illegality' and Deportability in Everyday Life." *Annual Review of Anthropology* 31: 419–47.

———. 2005a "Deportability, Detainability, and the Politics of Space in the Aftermath of 'Homeland Security.'" Homelands, Borders, and Trade in Latin America: Freedom, Violence, and Exchange after 9/11, Center for Iberian and Latin American Studies, University of California–San Diego, La Jolla, CA.

———. 2005b. *Working the Boundaries: Race, Space, and "Illegality" in Mexican Chicago*. Durham, NC: Duke University Press.

De Genova, Nicholas, and Nathalie Peutz, eds. 2010. *The Deportation Regime: Sovereignty, Space, and the Freedom of Movement*. Durham, NC: Duke University Press.

DeSipio, Louis, and Rodolfo O. de la Garza. 1998. *Making Americans, Remaking America: Immigration and Immigrant Policy*. Boulder, CO: Westview Press.

Dolnick, Sam. 2011. "U.S. Returns Young Girl, a Citizen, to Guatemala." *New York Times*, March 22.

Donato, Katharine M. 1993. "Current Trends and Patterns of Female Migration: Evidence from Mexico." *International Migration Review* 27 (4): 748–71.

Donato, Katharine M., Donna Gabaccia, Jennifer Holdaway, Martin Manalansan IV, and Patricia R. Pessar. 2006. "A Glass Half Full? Gender in Migration Studies." *International Migration Review* 11 (1): 3–26.

Donato, Katherine M., Brandon Wagner, and Evelyn Patterson. 2008. "The Cat and Mouse Game at the Mexico-U.S. Border: Gendered Patterns and Recent Shifts." *International Migration Review* 42 (2): 330–59.

Draeger, Justin. 2007. "The Sins of their Fathers: Should Immigrant Children Be Penalized for their Parents' Actions?" *Student Aid Transcript* 18 (1): 42–48.

Dreby, Joanna. 2006. "Honor and Virtue: Mexican Parenting in Transnational Context." *Gender and Society* 20 (1): 32–59.

———. 2009. "Transnational Gossip." *Qualitative Sociology* 32: 1–20.

———. 2010. *Divided by Borders: Mexican Migrants and their Children*. Berkeley: University of California Press.

Ehrenreich, Barbara, and Arlie Russell Hochschild, eds. 2002. *Global Woman: Nannies, Maids, and Sex Workers in the New Economy*. New York: Henry Holt.

Engels, Frederick. 1942. *The Origin of the Family, Private Property and the State*. 7th ed. (1964). New York: International Publishers.

Ensor, Marisa O., and Elzbieta M. Goździak. 2010. *Children and Migration: At the Crossroads of Resiliency and Vulnerability*. New York: Palgrave.

Espiritu, Yen Le. 2003a. *Home Bound: Filipino American Lives Across Cultures, Communities, and Countries.* Berkeley: University of California Press.

———. 2003b. "'We Don't Sleep Around Like White Girls Do': Family, Culture, and Gender in Filipina American Lives." In *Gender and U.S. Immigration: Contemporary Trends,* edited by Pierrette Hondagneu-Sotelo, 263–84. Berkeley: University of California Press.

Faier, Lieba. 2007. "Filipina Migrants in Japan and their Professions of Love." *American Ethnologist* 24 (1): 148–62.

———. 2009. *Intimate Encounters: Filipina Women and the Remaking of Rural Japan.* Berkeley: University of California Press.

Faist, Thomas. 1997a. "From Common Questions to Common Concepts." In *International Migration, Immobility and Development: Multidisciplinary Perspectives,* edited by Tomas Hammar, Grete Brochmann, Kristof Tamas, and Thomas Faist, 247–76. Oxford: Berg.

———. 1997b. "The Crucial Meso-Level." In *International Migration, Immobility and Development: Multidisciplinary Perspectives,* edited by Tomas Hammar, Grete Brochmann, Kristof Tamas, and Thomas Faist, 187–217. Oxford: Berg.

Farmer, Paul. 2004. *Pathologies of Power: Health, Human Rights, and the New War on the Poor.* California Series in Public Anthropology 4. Berkeley: University of California Press.

Feld, Steven, and Keith H. Basso. 1996. *Senses of Place.* Santa Fe, NM: School of American Research Press.

Field, Les W. 1999. *The Grimace of Macho Raton: Artisans, Identity and Nation in Late Twentieth Century Western Nicaragua.* Durham, NC: Duke University Press.

Flores, William V. 1997. "Citizens vs. Citizenry: Undocumented Immigrants and Latino Cultural Citizenship." In *Latino Cultural Citizenship: Claiming Identity, Space, and Rights,* edited by William V. Flores and Rina Benmayor, 255–77. Boston: Beacon Press.

Flores, William V., and Rina Benmayor, eds. 1997. *Latino Cultural Citizenship: Claiming Identity, Space, and Rights.* Boston: Beacon Press.

Foner, Nancy, ed. 2009. *Across Generations: Immigrant Families in America.* New York: New York University Press.

Foucault, Michel. 1977. *Discipline and Punish: The Birth of the Prison.* Translated from the French by Alan Sheridan. New York: Pantheon Books.

Fouron, Georges, and Nina Glick Schiller. 2002. "The Generation of Identity: Redefining the Second Generation within a Transnational Social Field." In *The Changing Face of Home: The Transnational Lives of the Second Generation,* edited by Peggy Levitt and Mary C. Waters, 168–208. New York: Russell Sage Foundation.

Gabaccia, Donna, ed. 1992. *Seeking Common Ground: Multidisciplinary Studies of Immigrant Women in the United States.* Westport, CT: Greenwood Press.

———. 1994. *From the Other Side: Women, Gender, and Immigrant Life in the U.S., 1820–1990.* Bloomington: Indiana University Press.

Gamburd, Michele Ruth. 2000. *The Kitchen Spoon's Handle: Transnationalism and Sri Lanka's Migrant Housemaids.* Ithaca, NY: Cornell University Press.

Ginsberg, Faye, and Anna Lowenhaupt Tsing, eds. 1990. *Uncertain Terms: Negotiating Gender in American Culture.* Boston: Beacon Press.

Glick Schiller, Nina, Linda Basch, and Cristina Blanc-Szanton, eds. 1992. *Towards a Transnational Perspective on Migration: Race, Class, Ethnicity and Nationalism Reconsidered.* New York: New York Academy of Sciences.

———. 1995. "From Immigrant to Transnational Migrant: Theorizing Transnational Migration." *Anthropological Quarterly* 68 (1): 48–63.

Glick Schiller, Nina, and Georges Eugene Fouron. 2001. *Georges Woke Up Laughing: Long-Distance Nationalism and the Search for Home.* Durham, NC: Duke University Press.

Goldring, Luin. 2001. "The Gender and Geography of Citizenship in Mexico-U.S. Transnational Spaces." *Identities* 7 (4): 501–37.

Gómez-Peña, Guillermo. 1996. *The New World Border: Prophecies, Poems, and Loqueras for the End of the Century.* San Francisco: City Lights Books.

Gonzales, Roberto. 2011. "Learning to be Illegal: Undocumented Youth and Shifting Legal Contexts in the Transition to Adulthood." *American Sociological Review* 76 (4): 602–19.

González-López, Gloria. 2005. *Erotic Journeys: Mexican Immigrants and their Sex Lives.* Berkeley: University of California Press.

Gopinath, Gayatri. 2005. *Impossible Desires: Queer Diasporas and South Asian Public Cultures.* Durham, NC: Duke University Press.

Gordimer, Nadine. 2002. *The Pickup.* New York: Penguin.

Grasmuck, Sherri, and Patricia R. Pessar. 1991. *Between Two Islands: Dominican International Migration.* Berkeley: University of California Press.

Grewal, Inderpal, and Caren Kaplan, eds. 1994. *Scattered Hegemonies: Postmodernity and Transnational Feminist Practices.* Minneapolis: University of Minnesota Press.

Grossberg, Lawrence. 2005. *Caught in the Crossfire: Kids, Politics, and America's Future.* Boulder, CO: Paradigm Publishers.

Gupta, Akhil, and James Ferguson. 1997a. "Beyond 'Culture': Space, Identity, and the Politics of Difference." In *Culture, Power, Place: Explorations in Critical Anthropology,* edited by Akhil Gupta and James Ferguson, 33–51. Durham, NC: Duke University Press.

———. 1997b. *Culture, Power, Place: Explorations in Critical Anthropology.* Durham, NC: Duke University Press.

Gutiérrez, David, ed. 1996. *Between Two Worlds: Mexican Immigrants in the United States.* Wilmington, DE: Jaguar Books.

Gutmann, Matthew C. 1996. *The Meanings of Macho: Being a Man in Mexico City.* Berkeley: University of California Press.

———, ed. 2003. *Changing Men and Masculinities in Latin America.* Durham, NC: Duke University Press.

Hammar, Tomas, Grete Brochmann, Kristof Tamas, and Thomas Faist, eds. 1997. *International Migration, Immobility and Development: Multidisciplinary Perspectives.* Oxford: Berg.

Hammar, Tomas, and Kristof Tamas. 1997. "Why Do People Go or Stay?" In *International Migration, Immobility and Development: Multidisciplinary Perspectives,* edited by Tomas Hammar, Grete Brochmann, Kristof Tamas, and Thomas Faist, 1–19. Oxford: Berg.

Haraway, Donna. 1986. "Primatology is Politics by Other Means." In *Feminist Approaches to Science,* edited by Ruth Bleier, 77–118. New York: Pergamon Press.

Hastrup, Kirsten, and Karen Fog Olwig. 1997. "Introduction." In *Siting Culture: The Shifting Anthropological Object,* edited by Karen Fog Olwig and Kirsten Hastrup, 1–14. London: Routledge.

Hawkins, Brian, Yedid Minjares, Lauren Harris, and Juan Rodríguez de la Gala. 2010. "Values in Conflict: Youth in a Culture of Migration." In *Mexican Migration and the U.S. Economic Crisis: A Transnational Perspective,* edited by Wayne A. Cornelius, David Fitzgerald, Pedro Lewin Fischer, and Leah Muse-Orlinoff, 161–84. San Diego: Center for Comparative Immigration Studies, University of California–San Diego.

Hellman, Judith Adler. 2008. *The World of Mexican Migrants: The Rock and the Hard Place.* New York: The New Press.

Hess, Julia Meredith. 2009. *Immigrant Ambassadors: Citizenship and Belonging in the Tibetan Diaspora.* Stanford, CA: Stanford University Press.

Hess, Julia Meredith, and Dianna Shandy. 2008. "Kids at the Crossroads: Global Childhood and the State." *Anthropological Quarterly* 81 (4): 765–76.

Heyman, Josiah McC. 1995. "Putting Power into the Anthropology of Bureaucracy: The Immigration and Naturalization Service at the Mexico-United States Border." *Current Anthropology* 36 (2): 261–87.

———. 1999a. "State Escalation of Force: A Vietnam/US-Mexico Border Analogy." In *States and Illegal Practices,* edited by Josiah Heyman, 285–314. Oxford: Berg.

———. 1999b. "United States Surveillance over Mexican Lives at the Border: Snapshots of an Emerging Regime." *Human Organization* 58 (4): 429–37.

———, ed. 1999c. *States and Illegal Practices.* Oxford: Berg.

———. 2000. "Respect for Outsiders? Respect for the Law? The Moral Evaluation of High-Scale Issues by US Immigration Officers." *Journal of the Royal Anthropological Institute* 6 (4): 635–52.

———. 2002. "U.S. Immigration Officers of Mexican Ancestry as Mexican Americans, Citizens, and Immigration Police." *Current Anthropology* 43 (3): 479–507.

Hicken, Jonathan, Mollie Cohen, and Jorge Narvaez. 2010. "Double Jeopardy: How U.S. Enforcement Policies Shape Tunkaseño Migration." In *Mexican Migration and the U.S. Economic Crisis: A Transnational Perspective,* edited by Wayne A. Cornelius, David Fitzgerald, Pedro Lewin Fischer, and Leah Muse-Orlinoff, 47–92. San Diego: Center for Comparative Immigration Studies, University of California–San Diego.

Hirsch, Jennifer S. 1999. "En el Norte La Mujer Manda: Gender, Generation, and Geography in a Mexican Transnational Community." *American Behavioral Scientist* 42 (9): 1332–49.

———. 2003. *A Courtship After Marriage: Sexuality and Love in Mexican Transnational Families.* Berkeley: University of California Press.

Hochschild, Arlie Russell. 2002. "Love and Gold." In *Global Woman: Nannies, Maids, and Sex Workers in the New Economy,* edited by Barbara Ehrenreich and Arlie Russell Hochschild, 15–30. New York: Henry Holt.

Hondagneu-Sotelo, Pierrette. 1994. *Gendered Transitions: Mexican Experiences of Immigration.* Berkeley: University of California Press.

———. 1999a. "Introduction: Gender and Contemporary U.S. Immigration." *American Behavioral Scientist* 42 (4): 565–76.

———, ed. 1999b. "Gender and Contemporary U.S. Immigration." Special Issue, *American Behavioral Scientist* 42 (4).

———. 2003a. "Gender and Immigration: A Retrospective and Introduction." In *Gender and U.S. Immigration: Contemporary Trends,* edited by Pierrette Hondagneu-Sotelo, 3–19. Berkeley: University of California Press.

———, ed. 2003b. *Gender and U.S. Immigration: Contemporary Trends*. Berkeley: University of California Press.

———. 2007. *Doméstica: Immigrant Workers Cleaning and Caring in the Shadows of Affluence*. Berkeley: University of California Press.

Hondagneu-Sotelo, Pierrette, and Ernestine Avila. 1997. "'I'm Here, but I'm There': The Meanings of Latina Transnational Motherhood." *Gender and Society* 11:548–71.

Inda, Jonathan Xavier, and Renato Rosaldo. 2008. *The Anthropology of Globalization: A Reader*. Oxford: Blackwell Publishing.

Jacobson, David. 1996. *Rights across Borders: Immigration and the Decline of Citizenship*. Baltimore, MD: Johns Hopkins University Press.

Jonas, Susanne. 1996. "Rethinking Immigration Policy and Citizenship in the Americas: A Regional Framework." *Social Justice* 23 (3): 68–85.

Jones-Correa, Michael. 1998. *Between Two Nations: The Political Predicament of Latinos in New York City*. Ithaca, NY: Cornell University Press.

Joseph, Gilbert M., and Daniel Nugent, eds. 1994. *Everyday Forms of State Formation: Revolution and the Negotiation of Rule in Modern Mexico*. Durham, NC: Duke University Press.

Kaplan, Caren, Norma Alarcón, and Minoo Moallem, eds. 1999. *Between Woman and Nation: Nationalisms, Transnational Feminisms, and the State*. Durham, NC: Duke University Press.

Kasinitz, Philip, John H. Mollenkopf, and Mary C. Waters, eds. 2004. *Becoming New Yorkers: Ethnographies of the New Second Generation*. New York: Russell Sage Foundation.

Kearney, Michael. 1991. "Borders and Boundaries of State and Self at the End of Empire." *Journal of Historical Sociology* 4:52–74.

———. 1995. "The Local and the Global: The Anthropology of Globalization and Transnationalism." *Annual Review of Anthropology* 24: 547–65.

———. 1996. *Reconceptualizing the Peasantry: Anthropology in Global Perspective*. Boulder, CO: Westview Press.

———. 1998. "Transnationalism in California and Mexico at the End of Empire." In *Border Identities: Nation and State at International Frontiers*, edited by Thomas M. Wilson and Hastings Donnan, 117–41. Cambridge: Cambridge University Press.

———. 2004. *Changing Fields of Anthropology: From Local to Global*. Rowman and Littlefield.

Knörr, Jacqueline. 2005. *Children and Migration: From Experience to Agency*. Verlag, Bielefeld: Transcript Press.

Kondo, Dorinne K. 1990. *Crafting Selves: Power, Gender, and Discourses of Identity in a Japanese Workplace*. Chicago: University of Chicago Press.

Lagarde y de los Rios, Marcela. 2003. *Los Cautiverios de las Mujeres: Madresposas, Monjas, Putas, Presas y Locas*. Coyoacán, D.F.: Universidad Nacional Autónoma de México.

Laguerre, Michel S. 1998. *Diasporic Citizenship: Haitian Americans in Transnational America*. New York: St. Martin's Press.

Lamphere, Louise. 1987. *From Working Daughters to Working Mothers: Immigrant Women in a New England Industrial Community*. Ithaca, NY: Cornell University Press.

———, ed. 1992. *Structuring Diversity: Ethnographic Perspectives on the New Immigration*. Chicago: University of Chicago Press.

Lamphere, Louise, Helena Ragoné, and Patricia Zavella, eds. 1997. *Situated Lives: Gender and Culture in Everyday Life*. New York: Routledge.

Latino USA. 2010. "American Dreamer: Sam." National Public Radio, February 19, 2010.

Lavie, Samdar, and Ted Swedenburg, eds. 1996. *Displacement, Diaspora and Geographies of Identity.* Durham, NC: Duke University Press.

Leinaweaver, Jessaca B. 2008. *The Circulation of Children: Kinship, Adoption, and Morality in Andean Peru.* Latin America Otherwise Series. Durham, NC: Duke University Press.

Levitt, Peggy. 2001. *The Transnational Villagers.* Berkeley: University of California Press.

Levitt, Peggy, and Mary C. Waters, eds. 2002. *The Changing Face of Home: The Transnational Lives of the Second Generation.* New York: Russell Sage Foundation.

Limón, José E. 1994. *Dancing with the Devil: Society and Cultural Poetics in Mexican-American South Texas.* Madison: The University of Wisconsin Press.

———. 1998. *American Encounters: Greater Mexico, the United States, and the Erotics of Culture.* Boston: Beacon Press.

Mahler, Sarah J. 2001. "Transnational Relationships: The Struggle to Communicate Across Borders." *Identities* 7 (4): 583–619.

———. 2003. "Engendering Transnational Migrations: A Case Study of Salvadorans." In *Gender and U.S. Immigration: Contemporary Trends,* edited by Pierrette Hondagneu-Sotelo, 287–316. Berkeley: University of California Press.

Mahler, Sarah J., and Patricia R. Pessar. 2001a. "Gendered Geographies of Power: Analyzing Gender Across Transnational Spaces." *Identities* 7 (4): 441–59.

———, eds. 2001b. "Gendering Transnational Spaces." Special Issue. *Identities* 7 (4).

———. 2006. "Gender Matters: Ethnographers Bring Gender from the Periphery toward the Core of Migration Studies." *International Migration Review* 40 (1): 27–63.

Maira, Sunaina. 2009. *Missing: Youth, Citizenship, and Empire after 9/11.* Durham, NC: Duke University Press.

Maira, Sunaina, and Elizabeth Soep, eds. 2005. *Youthscapes: The Popular, the National, the Global.* Philadelphia: University of Pennsylvania Press.

Malkin, Victoria. 2004. "'We Go to Get Ahead': Gender and Status in Two Mexican Migrant Communities." *Latin American Perspectives* 31 (5): 75–99.

Malkki, Liisa H. 1992. "National Geographic: The Rooting of Peoples and the Territorialization of National Identity among Scholars and Refugees." *Cultural Anthropology* 7 (1): 24–44.

Manalansan, Martin F. 2003. *Global Divas: Filipino Gay Men in the Diaspora.* Durham, NC: Duke University Press.

Marcus, George E. 1995. "Ethnography in/of the World System: The Emergence of Multi-Sited Ethnography." *Annual Review of Anthropology* 24: 95–117.

Maril, Robert Lee. 2004. *Patrolling Chaos: The U.S. Border Patrol in Deep South Texas.* Lubbock: Texas Tech University Press.

Martínez, Oscar J. 1994. *Border People: Life and Society in the U.S.-Mexico Borderlands.* Tucson: University of Arizona Press.

Massey, Douglas S., Jorge Durand, and Nolan J. Malone. 2002. *Beyond Smoke and Mirrors: Mexican Immigration in an Era of Economic Integration.* New York: Russell Sage Foundation.

Menjívar, Cecilia. 2000. *Fragmented Ties: Salvadoran Immigrant Ties in America.* Berkeley: University of California Press.

Menjívar, Cecilia, and Leisy Abrego. 2009. "Parents and Children across Borders: Legal Instability and Intergenerational Relations in Guatemalan and Salvadoran Families." In

Across Generations: Immigrant Families in America, edited by Nancy Foner, 160–89. New York: New York University Press.

Menjívar, Cecilia, and Olivia Salcido. 2002. "Immigrant Women and Domestic Violence: Common Experience in Different Countries." *Gender and Society* 16 (6): 898–920.

Minuteman Project. Website. http://www.minutemanproject.com/.

Miyoshi, Masao. 1993. "A Borderless World?: From Colonialism to Transnationalism and the Decline of the Nation State." *Critical Inquiry* 19: 726–51.

Mummert, Gail. 1994 "From *Metate* to *Despate*: Rural Mexican Women's Salaried Labor and the Redefinition of Gendered Spaces and Roles." In *Women of the Mexican Countryside, 1850–1990*, edited by Heather Fowler-Salamini and Mary Kay Vaughan, 192–209. Tucson: University of Arizona Press.

Nagengast, Carole. 1994. "Violence, Terror, and the Crisis of the State." *Annual Review of Anthropology* 23: 109–36.

Napolitano, Valentina. 2002. *Migration, Mujercitas, and Medicine Men: Living in Urban Mexico*. Berkeley: University of California Press.

Narayan, Uma. 1997. *Dislocating Cultures: Identities, Traditions, and Third World Feminism*. New York: Routledge.

Newendorp, Nicole. 2008. *Uneasy Reunions: Immigration, Citizenship, and Family Life in Post-1997 Hong Kong*. Stanford, CA: Stanford University Press.

Ngai, Mae M. 2004. *Impossible Subjects: Illegal Aliens and the Making of Modern America*. Princeton, NJ: Princeton University Press.

Nordstrom, Carolyn. 2004. *Shadows of War: Violence, Power, and International Profiteering in the Twenty-First Century*. California Series in Public Anthropology 10. Berkeley: University of California Press.

O'Leary, Anna Ochoa. 2009. "The ABCs of Migration Costs: Assembling, Bajadores, and Coyotes." *Migration Letters* 6 (1): 27–35.

Olwig, Karen Fog. 1997. "Cultural Sites: Sustaining a Home in a Deterritorialized World." In *Siting Culture: The Shifting Anthropological Object*, edited by Karen Fog Olwig and Kirsten Hastrup, 17–38. London: Routledge.

———. 2007. *Caribbean Journeys: An Ethnography of Migration and Home in Three Family Networks*. Durham, NC: Duke University Press.

Olwig, Karen Fog, and Kirsten Hastrup, eds. 1997. *Siting Culture: The Shifting Anthropological Object*. London: Routledge.

Ong, Aihwa. 1999. *Flexible Citizenship: The Cultural Logics of Transnationality*. Durham, NC: Duke University Press.

———. 2003. *Buddha Is Hiding: Refugees, Citizenship, the New America*. Berkeley: University of California Press.

Ong, Aihwa, and Stephen J. Collier. 2005. *Global Assemblages: Technology, Politics, and Ethics as Anthropological Problems*. Oxford: Blackwell Publishing.

Orellana, Marjorie Faulstich, Barrie Thorne, Anna Chee, and Wan Shun Eva Lam. 2001. "Transnational Childhoods: The Participation of Children in Processes of Family Migration." *Social Problems* 48 (4): 573–92.

Ortner, Sherry B. 1996. *Making Gender: The Politics and Erotics of Culture*. Boston: Beacon Press.

Padilla, Mark B., Jennifer S. Hirsch, Michael Munoz-Laboy, Robert Sember, and Richard G. Parker, eds. 2008. *Love and Globalization: Transformations of Intimacy in a Contemporary World.* Nashville, TN: Vanderbilt University Press.

Parreñas, Rhacel Salazar. 2001. *Servants of Globalization: Women, Migration, and Domestic Work.* Stanford, CA: Stanford University Press.

———. 2005. *Children of Global Migration: Transnational Families and Gendered Woes.* Stanford, CA: Stanford University Press.

———. 2008. *The Force of Domesticity: Filipina Migrants and Globalization.* New York: New York University Press.

Passel, Jeffrey S. 2005. "Estimates of the Size and Characteristics of the Undocumented Population." Washington, DC: Pew Hispanic Center.

Passel, Jeffrey S., and D'Vera Cohn. 2009. "A Portrait of Unauthorized Immigrants in the United States." Washington, DC: Pew Hispanic Center.

———. 2010. "Unauthorized Immigrant Population: National and State Trends, 2010." Washington, DC: Pew Hispanic Center.

Pessar, Patricia R. 1999. "Engendering Migration Studies: The Case of New Immigrants in the United States." *American Behavioral Scientist* 42 (4): 577–600.

———. 2003. "Engendering Migration Studies: The Case of New Immigrants in the United States." In *Gender and U.S. Immigration: Contemporary Trends,* edited by Pierrette Hondagneu-Sotelo, 20–42. Berkeley: University of California Press.

Pessar, Patricia R., and Sarah J. Mahler. 2003. "Transnational Migration: Bringing Gender In." *International Migration Review* 37 (3): 812–46.

Peutz, Nathalie. 2007. "Out-laws: Deportees, Desire, and 'The Law.'" *International Migration* 45 (3): 182–91.

Peutz, Nathalie, and Nicholas De Genova. 2010. "Introduction." In *The Deportation Regime: Sovereignty, Space, and the Freedom of Movement,* edited by Nicholas De Genova and Nathalie Peutz, 1–29. Durham, NC: Duke University Press.

Plascencia, Luis F. B. 2009. "The 'Undocumented' Mexican Migrant Question: Re-Examining the Framing of Law and Illegalization in the United States." *Urban Anthropology and Studies of Cultural Systems and World Economic Development* 38 (2–4): 375–434.

Pollock, Sheldon, Homi K. Bhabha, Carol A. Breckenridge, and Dipesh Chakrabary. 2002. "Cosmopolitanisms." In *Cosmopolitanism,* edited by Carol A. Breckenridge, Sheldon Pollock, Homi K. Bhabha, and Dipesh Chakrabarty, 1–19. Durham, NC: Duke University Press.

Portes, Alejandro, and Rubén G. Rumbaut. 2001. *Legacies: The Story of the Immigrant Second Generation.* Berkeley: University of California Press.

Povinelli, Elizabeth A. 2006. *The Empire of Love: Toward a Theory of Intimacy, Genealogy, and Carnality.* Durham, NC: Duke University Press.

Pozzetta, George E., ed. 1991. *Ethnicity and Gender: The Immigrant Woman.* New York: Garland.

Preston, Julia. 2007. "Immigration Quandary: A Mother Torn From Her Baby." *New York Times,* November 17.

———. 2008. "Perfectly Legal Immigrants, Until They Applied for Citizenship." *New York Times,* April 12.

———. 2009. "Illegal Immigrant Students Publicly Take Up Cause." *New York Times*, December 10.

Pribilsky, Jason. 2004. "'Aprendemos a Convivir': Conjugal Relations, Co-parenting, and Family Life among Ecuadorian Transnational Migrants in New York City and the Ecuadorian Andes." *Global Networks* 4 (3): 313–34.

———. 2007. *La Chula Vida: Gender, Migration, and Family in Andean Ecuador and New York City.* Syracuse, NY: Syracuse University Press.

Ramirez, Christian. 2005. "Militarization and Human Rights Violations on the U.S.-Mexico Border." Homelands, Borders and Trade in Latin America: Freedom, Violence, and Exchange After 9-11, Center for Iberian and Latin American Studies, University of California–San Diego, La Jolla, CA.

Rapport, Nigel, and Andre Dawson, eds. 1998. *Migrants of Identity: Perceptions of Home in a World of Movement.* Oxford: Berg.

Rebhun, L. A. 1999. The *Heart is Unknown Country: Love in the Changing Economy of Northeast Brazil.* Stanford, CA: Stanford University Press.

Rhodes, Lorna A. 2006. "Comments—Embarking on an Anthropology of Removal by Nathalie Peutz." *Current Anthropology* 47 (2): 235–37.

Rodríguez, Néstor. 1996. The Battle for the Border: Notes on Autonomous Migration, Transnational Communities, and the State. *Social Justice* 23 (3): 21–37.

Rosaldo, Michelle Z., and Louise Lamphere, eds. 1974. *Woman, Culture and Society.* Stanford, CA: Stanford University Press.

Rosaldo, Renato. 1997. "Cultural Citizenship, Inequality, and Multiculturalism." In *Latino Cultural Citizenship: Claiming Identity, Space, and Rights,* edited by William V. Flores and Rina Benmayor, 27–38. Boston: Beacon Press.

Rosaldo, Renato, and William V. Flores. 1997. "Identity, Conflict, and Evolving Latino Communities: Cultural Citizenship in San Jose, California." In *Latino Cultural Citizenship: Claiming Identity, Space, and Rights,* edited by William V. Flores and Rina Benmayor, 57–96. Boston: Beacon Press.

Rosas, Gilberto. 2007. "The Fragile Ends of War: Forging the United States-Mexico Border and Borderlands Consciousness." *Social Text* 91, 25 (2): 81–102.

Rouse, Roger. 1991. "Mexican Migration and the Social Space of Postmodernism." *Diaspora* 1 (1): 8–23.

———. 1992. "Making Sense of Settlement: Class Transformation, Cultural Struggle, and Transnationalism among Mexican Migrants in the United States." In *Towards a Transnational Perspective on Migration,* edited by Nina Glick Schiller, Linda Basch, and Cristina Blanc-Szanton, 25–52. New York: New York Academy of Sciences.

Rumbaut, Rubén G. 2004. "Ages, Life Stages, and Generational Cohorts: Decomposing the Immigrant First and Second Generations in the United States." *International Migration Review* 38: 1160–1205.

Rumbaut, Rubén G., and Alejandro Portes, eds. 2001. *Ethnicities: Children of Immigrants in America.* Berkeley: University of California Press.

Salcido, Olivia, and Madelaine Adelman. 2004. "'He Has Me Tied with the Blessed and Damned Papers': Undocumented-Immigrant Battered Women in Phoenix, Arizona." *Human Organization* 63 (2): 162–72.

Santa Ana, Otto. 2002. *Brown Tide Rising: Metaphors of Latinos in Contemporary American Public Discourse.* Austin: University of Texas Press.

Sargent, Lydia, ed. 1981. *Women and Revolution: A Discussion of the Unhappy Marriage of Marxism and Feminism.* Cambridge, MA: South End Press.

Sassen, Saskia. 1996a. "Beyond Sovereignty: Immigration Policy Making Today." *Social Justice* 23 (3): 9–20.

———. 1996b. "U.S. Immigration Policy toward Mexico in a Global Economy." In *Between Two Worlds: Mexican Immigrants in the United States,* edited by David Gutiérrez, 213–27. Wilmington, DE: Jaguar Books.

———. 1998. *Globalization and Its Discontents: Essays on the New Mobility of People and Money.* New York: The New Press.

———. 1999. *Guests and Aliens.* New York: The New Press.

Scheper-Hughes, Nancy, and Philippe Bourgois. 2004. "Introduction: Making Sense of Violence." In *Violence in War and Peace: An Anthology,* edited by Nancy Scheper-Hughes and Philippe Bourgois, 1–31. Oxford: Blackwell Publishing.

Schuck, Peter H. 1998. *Citizens, Strangers, and In-Betweens.* Boulder, CO: Westview Press.

Segura, Denise A., and Patricia Zavella, eds. 2007. *Women and Migration in the U.S.-Mexico Borderlands: A Reader.* Durham, NC: Duke University Press.

Shandy, Dianna. 2008. "Irish Babies and African Mothers: Rites of Passage and Rights in Citizenship in Post-Millenial Ireland." *Anthropological Quarterly* 81 (4): 803–81.

Sharma, Aradhana, and Akhil Gupta, eds. 2006. *The Anthropology of the State: A Reader.* Oxford: Blackwell Publishing.

Silva, Travis, Charlene Chang, Carmina Osuna, and Ivan Solís Sosa. 2010. "Leaving to Learn or Learning to Leave: Education in Tunkás." In *Mexican Migration and the U.S. Economic Crisis: A Transnational Perspective,* edited by Wayne A. Cornelius, David Fitzgerald, Pedro Lewin Fischer, and Leah Muse-Orlinoff, 131–58. San Diego: Center for Comparative Immigration Studies, University of California–San Diego.

Simon, Rita James, and Caroline Brettell, eds. 1986. *International Migration: The Female Experience.* Totowa, NJ: Rowman and Allanheld.

Sirkeci, Ibrahim. 2009. "Transnational Mobility and Conflict." *Migration Letters* 6 (1): 3–14.

Smith, Robert C. 2002. "Life Course, Generation, and Social Location as Factors Shaping Second-Generation Transnational Life." In *The Changing Face of Home: The Transnational Lives of the Second Generation,* edited by Peggy Levitt and Mary C. Waters, 145–67. New York: Russell Sage Foundation.

———. 2006. *Mexican New York: Transnational Lives of New Immigrants.* Berkeley: University of California Press.

Spener, David. 2009. *Clandestine Crossings: Migrants and Coyotes on the Texas-Mexico Border.* Ithaca, NY: Cornell University Press.

Stephen, Lynn. 1991. *Zapotec Women.* Austin: University of Texas Press.

———. 2003. "Cultural Citizenship and Labor Rights for Oregon Farmworkers: The Case of Pineros y Campesinos Unidos del Nordoeste (PCUN)." *Human Organization* 62 (1): 27–38.

———. 2007. *Transborder Lives: Indigenous Oaxacans in Mexico, California, and Oregon.* Durham, NC: Duke University Press.

Stevens, Jacqueline. 1999. *Reproducing the State.* Princeton, NJ: Princeton University Press.

Stewart, Mary White. 2001. *Ordinary Violence: Everyday Assaults Against Women*. Westport, CT: Bergin and Garvey.

Stoler, Ann Laura. 1995. *Race and the Education of Desire: Foucault's History of Sexuality and the Colonial Order of Things*. Durham, NC: Duke University Press.

———. 2002. *Carnal Knowledge and Imperial Power*. Berkeley: University of California Press.

Terrio, Susan. 2008. "New Barbarians at the Gates of Paris?: Prosecuting Undocumented Minors in the Juvenile Court—The Problem of the 'Petits Roumains.'" *Anthropological Quarterly* 81 (4): 873–901.

Thompson, Ginger, and Marc Lacey. 2009. "Obama Arrives in Mexico for Start of Summit." *New York Times*, August 10.

Thorne, Barrie, Marjorie Faulstich Orellana, Wan Shun Eva Lam, and Anna Chee. 2003. "Raising Children, and Growing Up across National Borders: Comparative Perspectives on Age, Gender, and Migration. In *Gender and U.S. Immigration: Contemporary Trends*, edited by Pierrette Hondagneu-Sotelo, 241–62. Berkeley: University of California Press.

Thorne, Barrie, and Marilyn Yalom. 1992. *Rethinking the Family: Some Feminist Questions*. Boston: Northeastern University Press.

Tsing, Anna Lowenhaupt. 1993. *In the Realm of the Diamond Queen: Marginality in an Out-of-the-Way Place*. Princeton, NJ: Princeton University Press.

———. 2005. *Friction: An Ethnography of Global Connection*. Princeton, NJ: Princeton University Press.

Turnovsky, Carolyn Pinedo. 2006. "A La Parada: The Social Practices of Men on a Street Corner." *Social Text* 88, 24 (3): 55–72.

Uehling, Greta. 2008. "The International Smuggling of Children: Coyotes, Snakeheads and the Politics of Compassion." *Anthropological Quarterly* 8 (41): 833–71.

United States Department of Homeland Security. 2008. *Yearbook of Immigration Statistics: 2007*. Washington, DC: U.S. Department of Homeland Security, Office of Immigration Statistics.

———. 2010. *Yearbook of Immigration Statistics: 2009*. Washington, DC: U.S. Department of Homeland Security, Office of Immigration Statistics.

United States Immigration and Customs Enforcement. 2007. Press release. http://www.ice.gov/pi/news/newsreleases/articles/070821dc.htm

Vélez-Ibáñez, Carlos G. 1996. *Border Visions: Mexican Cultures of the Southwest United States*. Tucson: University of Arizona Press.

Vertovec, Steven. 2009. *Transnationalism*. London: Routledge.

Vila, Pablo. 2000. *Crossing Borders, Reinforcing Borders: Social Categories, Metaphors, and Narrative Identities on the U.S.-Mexico Frontier*. Austin: University of Texas Press.

———. 2005. *Border Identifications: Narratives of Religion, Gender, and Class on the U.S.-Mexico Border*. Austin: University of Texas Press.

Villalón, Roberta. 2010. *Violence Against Latina Immigrants: Citizenship, Inequality, and Community*. New York: New York University Press.

Werner, Cynthia, and Holly R. Barcus. 2009. "Mobility and Immobility in a Transnational Context: Changing Views of Migration among the Kazakh Diaspora in Mongolia." *Migration Letters* 6 (1): 49–62.

Willen, Sarah S. 2007. "Exploring 'Illegal' and 'Irregular' Migrants' Lived Experiences of Law and State Power." *International Migration* 45 (3): 2–7.

Wilson, Ara. 2004. *The Intimate Economies of Bangkok: Tomboys, Tycoons, and Avon Ladies in the Global City*. Berkeley: University of California Press.

Wilson, Tamar Diana. 2000. "Anti-Immigrant Sentiment and the Problem of Reproduction/Maintenance in Mexican Immigration to the United States. *Critique of Anthropology* 20 (2): 191–213.

———. 2006. "Strapping the Mexican Woman Immigrant: The Convergence of Reproduction and Production." *Anthropological Quarterly* 79 (2): 295–302.

———. 2009. *Women's Migration Networks in Mexico and Beyond*. Albuquerque: University of New Mexico Press.

Wilson, Thomas M., and Hastings Donnan, eds. 1998. *Border Identities: Nation and State at International Frontiers*. Cambridge: Cambridge University Press.

Yaeger, Patricia, ed. 1996. *The Geography of Identity*. Ann Arbor: University of Michigan Press.

Yuval-Davis, Nira, and Floya Anthias, eds. 1989. *Woman-Nation-State*. London: Macmillan.

Yuval-Davis, Nira, and Pnina Werbner, eds. 1999. *Women, Citizenship and Difference*. London: Zed Books.

Zimmerman, Mary K., Jacquelyn S. Litt, and Christine E. Bose, eds. 2006. *Global Dimensions of Gender and Carework*. Stanford, CA: Stanford University Press.

Index

Lucía, 2–3, 24, 31, 51, 144
Luis, 49
Luisa, 96–97
Luna family, 35–37
Lupe, 83–84

Magdalena, 78
Male adolescents, 115–16; patriarchal rites of passage, 121–22, 125–26
Male dominance, 87–88; commentary about, 85; long-distance, 82
Male identity, 75
Malkki, Liisa, 50
Mapping intimate migrations, 10–14
María, 50
Mariela, 9–10
Marisa, 57–58, 59
Marriage, 39, 58, 59; migration after, 73–75; transforming roles within, 71
Marta, 87
Martín, 74–75
Masculinity, 72, 146; exaggerated displays of, 77; legal status and, 73–80; in U.S., 77–80, 85–86; violence and, 75–76
Mateo, 59
Mauricio, 98–99
Mayra, 122–23
Melina, Bella, 137–38
Melina, Cristo, 137–38
Melina, Lety, 137–38
Melina, Vito, 138
Men: controls on, 107; female migration controlled by, 96; households of, 42–43; infidelity and, 104; kin relations extended, 43; labor on farms, 44, 73; masculinities and shifting status of, 73–80; *por la tierra* (by land), 98–99; power imbalances and, 72; social critique by, 78; violence between, 76–77. *See also* Male dominance; Masculinity
Mercedes, 117–18
Metaphorical place, 49–50
Mexican nationals, repatriation of (1920s and 1930s), 14
Microborders, 93
Migrant. *See* Immigrants

Migration, 9, 18, 19; age and gender structuring, 111–12; autonomous, 65–66; autonomy lost, 77–78; circuit established, 34, 36, 39; community building after, 47; family relations supporting, 33, 58; flow and notions of family, 11, 33–34; generation structuring, 111–12; after marriage, 73–75; motivation for, 118–19, 132–33; as patriarchal rite of passage, 121–22; patrilocality and, 45–46; studies, 12; women impacted by, 72. *See also* Child migration; Female migration; Gendered migration; Undocumented migration
Miguel, 81, 102
Militarization, of border, 3, 63, 99
Mitad allá, mitad aquí (half there, half here), 6, 31–51, 144
Mixed-status families, 61–67, 137
Moisés, 40
Moreno family, 38–41
Mothers-in-law, 42–43
Mummert, Gail, 89

Narayan, Uma, 76
Natel, Kelly, 132
Nation, home as, 47–49
National belonging, 48
National Council of La Raza, 134–35
National membership, 131, 147
National-origin quotas, 16
Naturalization, 15–16, 59, 128; deportation during, 150; swearing-in ceremony, 64–65
Ngai, Mae M., 128, 134, 136
Ni de aquí, ni de allá (from neither here nor there), 6, 143
Nina, 116–17, 135
Non-migration. *See* Immobility (or non-migration)

Obama, Barack, 151
Ofelia, 1–2, 25, 143, 144, 147, 149, 151
Ong, Aihwa, 144
Operation Wetback (1954), 14
Ortner, Sherry B., 17
Oscar, 137

About the Author

DEBORAH A. BOEHM is Assistant Professor of Anthropology and Women's Studies and a faculty associate in the Gender, Race, and Identity Program at the University of Nevada, Reno. She is co-editor of *Everyday Ruptures: Children, Youth, and Migration in Global Perspective.*

CPSIA information can be obtained
at www.ICGtesting.com
Printed in the USA
JSHW051929161221
21313JS00006B/165